Educational Technology Program and Project Evaluation

Educational Technology Program and Project Evaluation is a unique, comprehensive guide to the formative and summative evaluation of projects, programs, products, practices, and policies involving educational technology. Written for both beginning and experienced evaluators, the book utilizes an integrative, systems-based approach; its practical emphasis on logic models and theories of change will help readers navigate their own evaluation processes to improve interventions and conduct meaningful educational research. Key features include:

- evidence-based guidelines for constructing and conducting evaluations
- practical exercises to support the development of knowledge, skills, and program evaluation portfolios
- a variety of interdisciplinary case studies
- references and links to pertinent research and resources

Using the TELL, ASK, SHOW, DO model first introduced in this series, *Educational Technology Program and Project Evaluation* provides comprehensive coverage of the concepts, goals, design, implementation, and critical questions imperative to successful technology-enhanced evaluation.

J. Michael Spector is Professor and former Chair of the Department of Learning Technologies at the University of North Texas, USA. Dr. Spector has served as Executive Vice President on the International Board of Standards for Training, Performance and Instruction (ibstpi), a member of the Executive Committee of the IEEE Computer Society's Learning Technology Technical Committee, and as President of the Association for Educational and Communications Technology (AECT). He was lead editor on the third and fourth editions of the *Handbook of Research on Educational Communications and Technology*, edited the *Encylopedia of Educational Technology*, and has more than 150 journal articles, book chapters, and books to his credit.

Allan H.K. Yuen is Associate Professor, Director of the Centre for Information Technology in Education, and Program Director of the B.Sc. in Information Management in the Division of Information and Technology Studies at the University of Hong Kong. Dr. Yuen is the Editor of the *Journal of Communication and Education* and has more than 100 publications including journal articles, book chapters, and books. He has served as Vice Chairman of the Hong Kong Educational Research Association (HKERA), and as President of the Hong Kong Association for Educational Communications and Technology (HKAECT).

Interdisciplinary Approaches to Educational Technology

Series Editor: J. Michael Spector

Current and forthcoming series titles:

Educational Technology Program and Project Evaluation

J. MICHAEL SPECTOR
ALLAN H.K. YUEN

Routledge
Taylor & Francis Group

NEW YORK AND LONDON

First published 2016
by Routledge
711 Third Avenue, New York, NY 10017

and by Routledge
2 Park Square, Milton Park, Abingdon, Oxon OX14 4RN

Routledge is an imprint of the Taylor & Francis Group, an informa business

© 2016 Taylor & Francis

The right of J. Michael Spector and Allan H.K. Yuen to be identified as the authors of this work
has been asserted by them in accordance with sections 77 and 78 of the Copyright, Designs
and Patents Act 1988.

Trademark notice: Product or corporate names may be trademarks or registered trademarks,
and are used only for identification and explanation without intent to infringe.

Library of Congress Cataloging-in-Publication Data
Names: Spector, J. Michael, author. | Yuen, Allan, author.
Title: Educational technology program and project evaluation/J. Michael Spector, Allan H.K. Yuen.
Description: New York: Routledge, 2016. | Series: Interdisciplinary approaches to educational technology |
    Includes bibliographical references and index.
Identifiers: LCCN 2015038117| ISBN 9781138851412 (hardback) | ISBN 9781138851429 (pbk.) |
    ISBN 9781315724140 (ebook)
Subjects: LCSH: Educational technology—Evaluation. | Computer-assisted instruction—Evaluation. |
    School management and organization. | Project management.
Classification: LCC LB1028.3 .S6294 2016 | DDC 371.33—dc23
LC record available at http://lccn.loc.gov/2015038117

ISBN: 978-1-138-85141-2 (hbk)
ISBN: 978-1-138-85142-9 (pbk)
ISBN: 978-1-315-72414-0 (ebk)

Typeset in Minion Pro, Helvetica Neue and Copperplate Gothic
by Florence Production Ltd, Stoodleigh, Devon, UK

Printed and bound in the United States of America by
Edwards Brothers Malloy on sustainably sourced paper

This volume is dedicated to our many mentors, especially Professor Robert M. Gagné (deceased), internationally recognized scholar in educational psychology and instructional systems, and Professor and founding leader of the Hong Kong Association for Educational Communications and Technology, Leo P. K. Yam (retired).

Contents

Preface

The general goals of **education** include developing (a) basic knowledge and skills, (b) productive work competencies, (c) critical thinking and higher order reasoning skills, (d) the capacity for and interest in lifelong **learning**, and (e) responsible and thoughtful citizens (Spector, 2016). These goals are emphasized and prioritized differently at different times and places and with different learners and learning tasks.

We begin with this general remark about goals because goals, objectives and intentions are the motivation for and inform efforts to develop effective and efficient learning activities and environments and associated instructional resources and systems. Many such efforts involve the use and integration of various kinds of **technology**, including such things as specific learning applications, mobile devices, augmented realities, course and learning management systems, algorithms to assess student progress, rubrics for grading assignments, automated feedback mechanisms for activities, and much more.

This is an era especially rich in terms of available and affordable resources that can be used to support learning, **performance** and **instruction**. As a consequence, deciding which educational technology applications and practices work best in various situations is an increasingly challenging task for designers, developers, instructors, students, parents, administrators, funding agencies and policymakers. The general goals of educational technology evaluation are (a) to aid in the design, development and deployment of effective and efficient educational technologies, and (b) to provide relevant constituencies with evidence of what works best, when, where, why and how. The purpose of this volume is to help develop the capacity of educational technology evaluators to perform those two functions well.

This volume is divided into five parts, each of which aims to develop specific knowledge and skills in targeted areas. Each of these parts is briefly discussed next. The additional resources in Part V include a glossary of terms, consolidated references, a sample draft evaluation plan, professional associations, and a list of evaluation journals.

Part I: Introduction and Overview

The first part of this volume includes five chapters aimed at providing foundation knowledge for the remaining parts. The topics covered include the nature of learning, performance and instruction (Chapter 1), an overview of **projects**, **programs**, **products**, **practice** and **policies** (Chapter 2), the typical goals and scope of evaluations (Chapter 3), the various types of evaluations and evaluators (Chapter 4), and the major tasks involved in an evaluation (Chapter 5). Many of the ideas introduced in Part I are elaborated in subsequent parts of the volume.

Part II: An Evaluation Framework

The second part of this volume presents an evaluation framework that is used throughout the book. Each part of the framework is elaborated separately, beginning with **needs assessment** (Chapter 6), since it is important to understand the problem and needs before engaging in an educational technology effort. Once the problem and needs are identified, it is then important to investigate the likely causes so as to get beyond the superficial symptoms of the problem (Chapter 7). The notion of an educational technology effort, or most any **educational intervention**, is to transform a problematic situation into a desirable situation; the justification for that process is called a **theory of change** (Chapter 8). The outcomes of the effort and how they are to be measured should link back to the identified problem and underlying causes (Chapter 9). Part II concludes with a discussion of things that might be especially challenging or detract from achieving the intended outcomes—namely, **mediators**, **moderators** and contextual factors (Chapter 10).

Part III: Logic Models and Implementations

The third part of the volume addresses the primary tools and methods involved in conducting evaluations. The theory of change introduced in Part II is critical in planning interventions and the associated indicators of success (Chapter 11). A theory of change can be represented visually in the form of a **logic model** (Chapter 12) that depicts the problem situation, input variables and factors, **output** indicators of the intervention and planned support, and the short-, medium- and long-term outcomes of a successful intervention (Chapter 13). Issues involved in developing, validating and using instruments, and following protocols to ensure **reliability** are discussed (Chapter 14). Fidelity of implementation (a typical kind of **formative evaluation**) is treated separately

(Chapter 15) as it is the most critical aspect of an evaluation in that explaining the extent to which an effort achieves intended outcomes (**summative evaluation**) requires a robust formative evaluation effort and associated evidence.

Part IV: Translating Plans into Action

The fourth part of this volume is focused on applying the knowledge and principles previously elaborated. Milestones for the effective integration of technology are treated (Chapter 16) as these set a clear path to follow from the problem identification stage to the implementation and deployment stage of an effort. The value and ways of conducting multiple formative evaluations of an effort as it evolves are addressed (Chapter 17) as there are many things that can contribute to or detract from the success of an effort. The need to address potential pitfalls and problems is critical for success (Chapter 18), and adjusting the implementation plan for an effort may be a positive outcome of a formative evaluation. The kinds of data to be collected and analyzed in an evaluation vary with the nature of the effort and include both qualitative and quantitative data (Chapter 19). Linking evaluations to practice and policy is one of the most important outcomes of an evaluation (Chapter 20), and doing so requires careful and thorough documentation and reporting of the effort (Chapter 21).

Part V: Additional Resources

This part of the volume includes a glossary of key terms, a consolidated list of references cited in the first four parts, a partially complete sample evaluation plan, refereed evaluation journals, and a list of evaluation associations.

Each of the chapters in the first four parts is structured to provide introductory remarks followed by a discussion of the major points covered. There are activities and quizzes embedded throughout the chapters. Each of the major chapters concludes with a major challenge that might be taken up as part of a small group project or included in an individual portfolio being constructed in association with a course and the use of this textbook. Many things discussed in the first volume in this series, *Foundations of Educational Technology: Integrative Approaches and Interdisciplinary Perspectives* (2nd ed.) (Spector, 2016), are revisited and reinforced in this volume.

This is by no means a definitive treatise on educational technology project and program evaluation. It is intended to be a useful textbook to help orient those new to the area of evaluating educational technology efforts. A particular challenge addressed in this volume involves the complexity of learning environments and instructional systems to which specific educational technologies are intended to contribute. That complexity is a result of such things as ill-defined and dynamic goals and objectives, the variety of knowledge and skills to be developed, the incredible number and variety of Internet-based resources that can be used to support learning and instruction, and many significant differences among learners, instructors, technical specialists, administrators and decision makers (e.g., prior knowledge, preferences, language, culture, perspectives, values, etc.). The wealth of resources now available along with the variety of learning tasks, learners and levels of learning, make the task of planning and implementing effective instruction very challenging. That challenge makes the task of educational technology evaluation more important than ever before.

When asked, many will say that education is important and that education can be improved. We can do better. Many also believe that to improve learning and instruction in a systematic and sustained manner what is needed is better teacher training and professional development, more effective learning activities and support, and more flexible and adaptive technologies (Spector, 2016).

As a result, many efforts to improve education involve the use or integration of educational technology. Those efforts, which can take the form of a program, project, product, practice or policy, need to be designed with a clear understanding of (a) the problem situation or context, (b) specific goals and objectives, (c) relevant research and theory, (d) constraints and conditions, and (e) what has worked well in similar situations. Design and development are obviously challenging.

Evaluating what has been designed and developed is even more challenging, in our opinion. Given the costs involved in an educational technology effort, and the importance of the general goal to improve learning and instruction, it does not make good sense to wait until an effort has been completed or put into use to begin an evaluation. The evaluation should begin with the situation analysis and continue through design, development and deployment. Why? Because it is important to make the best possible effort to attain the intended goals. If the effort fails to achieve the intended goals and objectives, then precious time, effort and resources will have been wasted.

For this reason, this book proceeds based on the notion that there are two tasks to be performed by evaluators: (1) *help the effort succeed* (formative evaluation) by being involved throughout the process and providing feedback and consulting from an independent but constructive perspective, and (2) *report the extent to which the effort succeeded* (summative evaluation). This volume is unique in that it includes educational products, practices and policies as well as projects and programs as efforts that could and should be evaluated.

There are of course other good books in the area of program and project evaluation. A few of these related resources published since 2000 include:

- *Method of Evaluating Educational Technology* by Walt Heinecke and Laura Blasi, published in 2001 by Information Age Publishing; somewhat dated with regard to technologies, but strong on methodologies;
- *Assessing the Impact of Technology in Teaching and Learning: A Sourcebook for Evaluators* by Jerome Johnston and Linda Toms Barker, funded by the US Department of Education and published by the Institute for Social Research at the University of Michigan in 2002, and available at www.rcgd.isr.umich.edu/tlt/ TechSbk.pdf;

- *Evaluation and Assessment in Educational Information Technology* edited by Leping Liu, D. Lamont Johnson, Cleborne D. Maddux and Norma Henderson, published by Hawthorne Press in 2001.
- Models and Methods of Evaluation by Ronald Owston, published in 2008 in the *Handbook of Research on Educational Communications and Technology* (3rd ed.) by Taylor & Francis; available at www.mums.ac.ir/shares/meddept/meddept/ E-Books/Handbook%20of%20Research%20on%20Educational%20Communications %20and%20Technology.pdf;
- *Instructional Technology/Evaluation of IT as a Profession*, a Wikibook available under the Creative Commons Attribution at www.en.wikibooks.org/wiki/Instructional_ Technology/Evaluation_of_IT_as_a_profession and updated in 2013;
- *Educational Technology: Knowledge Assessment* by Marmar Mukhopadhayay (Ed.), published by Shipra in 2014;
- Program and Project Evaluation by J. Michael Spector, published by Springer in 2014 in the *Handbook of Research on Educational Communications and Technology* (4th ed.); available at www.link.springer.com/chapter/10.1007/978-1-4614-3185- 5_16#page-1;
- Planning a Program Evaluation: Matching Methodology to Program Status by Jennifer Hamilton and Jill Feldman, in the 2014 *Handbook of Research on Educational Communications and Technology* (4th ed.); available at www.link. springer.com/chapter/10.1007/978-1-4614-3185-5_2.

In addition to these resources on educational technology evaluation, there are several excellent books that cover the research, theory and design context in which educational technology efforts occur, including:

- *The Instructional Design Knowledge Base: Theory, Research and Practice* by Rita C. Richey, James D. Klein and Monica W. Tracey, published in 2010 by Routledge/ Taylor & Francis;
- *Handbook of Practical Program Evaluation* (3rd ed.) by Joseph S. Wholey, Harry P. Hatry and Kathryn E. Newcomer (Eds.), published in 2010 by Jossey-Bass/Wiley;
- *WHO Evaluation Practice Handbook* by the World Health Organization in 2013 to streamline WHO evaluation; available at www.apps.who.int/iris/bitstream/10 665/96311/1/9789241548687_eng.pdf;
- *Streamlined ID: A Practical Guide to Instructional Design* by Miriam Larson and Barbara B. Lockee, published in 2013 by Routledge/Taylor & Francis.

Resources

Steps to Evaluate the Value of Educational Technology—initial, high-level guide provided by Teachnology, available at www.teach-nology.com/teachers/educational_technology/evaluation/

Evaluation of Education Technology: What We Know and What Can We Know—1995 Rand Corporation Report by Douglas C. Merrill, available at www.rand.org/content/dam/rand/pubs/drafts/2008/DRU1049.pdf

Evaluation of Educational Technologies—University of Warwick Website with many resources (guides, case studies, tools, etc.), available at https://web.warwick.ac.uk/ETS/Resources/evaluation.htm

References

Spector, J. M. (2016). *Foundations of educational technology: Integrative approaches and interdisciplinary perspectives* (2nd ed.). New York: Routledge.

Acknowledgments

We wish to thank many people who have provided insight and feedback to us during the planning and writing stage. We are especially grateful to Milton C. Nielsen (Texas State University) and Wilhelmina Savenye (Arizona State University) who provided feedback on various parts of this volume and who are also contributing to this textbook series. We also thank Alex Masulis, senior editor at Routledge, for his patience and guidance throughout the process.

part one

INTRODUCTION AND OVERVIEW

one
The Nature of Learning, Performance and Instruction

Hence the central problem of an education based upon experience is to select the kind of present experiences that live fruitfully and creatively in subsequent experiences.
(*from John Dewey's* Experience and Education)

As reported elsewhere (Spector, 2012, 2016), M. David Merrill was fond of saying that people learn what they do. There is a natural link between doing and learning, as implied by the opening quotation by Dewey (1938). Many instructional design practitioners and researchers realize that natural connection and have argued for instructional approaches that integrate human performance on realistic tasks. These approaches include anchored instruction (CTGV, 1990), authentic learning (Blumenfeld et al., 1991), cognitive apprenticeship (Collins, Brown, & Newman, 1987), and situated learning (Lave & Wenger, 1990), among others.

Instructional designers and educational researchers generally accept the premise that people learn what they do. This premise resonates well with popular beliefs, such as *practice makes perfect*, as well as with neural science and how repetition can result in neural reinforcement and explain how some procedural activities become automatic after many repetitions by a person. Accepting that premise has strong implications for both design and **evaluation**. For design, it means that it is important to include in an instructional sequence the actions and activities that are pertinent to the targeted competencies and skills (e.g., authentic tasks). For evaluation, the implications are that these two things are important: (a) the degree to which the selected actions and activities are appropriately linked to the targeted competencies and skills, and then (b) the degree to which learners are able to develop those competencies and skills.

As a consequence, designers and evaluators have a strong interest in needs assessment, problem definition and requirements analysis. Both designers and evaluators generally start with questions that address what people now know and are able to do, and then what knowledge, skills and understanding they should develop with appropriate education, training and experience. As typically happens, technology is involved in the education, training and experience that is intended to take an individual or group of individuals from one state of understanding or level of performance to a higher state or level.

Design and development play a critical role in the process of promoting knowledge and understanding, developing skills and improving performance. Instructors, tutors and coaches also play critical and well-acknowledged roles in that process, as do technical specialists and other support personnel. Less well acknowledged in many cases, is the vital role played by evaluators in the processes associated with planning and implementing solutions aimed at improving knowledge, understanding and performance. This book is about the vital roles that evaluators play and the value they add to progress in using technology effectively and efficiently in support of learning, instruction and performance.

We begin with definitions and reminders presented in the *Foundations* volume in this series. We then put the key concepts of learning, performance and instruction together in a context involving educational technology and conclude with a representative challenge.

Learning

Defining learning

The classical view of a definition involves the essence of the thing being defined—that which makes it what it is and not something else. One might be tempted to ask about the essence of learning. What is it that counts as evidence of learning as opposed to something else, such as evidence of enthusiasm or evidence of short-term recall or evidence of appreciation for a teacher?

The definition of learning introduced in the *Foundations* volume (Spector, 2012, 2016) addresses a process view of learning, as opposed to an event or product view—namely, learning is a process that is aimed at stable and persistent changes in what an individual or a group of individuals know and can do. Indicators of success include relevant (in terms of contributing to intended outcomes) changes in abilities, attitudes, beliefs, knowledge, **mental models**, motivation, skills, and so on.

There are several critical aspects of this definition that have implications for evaluation. The first is the fundamental notion of change. Without reliable indicators of relevant change, there is no evidence of success. An early task for an evaluator (or evaluation team) is to identify the targeted changes and help those involved develop credible ways to detect, document and report changes. Another early task of an evaluator is to be sure that the indicated changes to be monitored and reported are clearly linked to the intended outcomes of the effort. These early tasks are part of an evaluator's responsibility to help an effort achieve intended outcomes. In too many cases, an evaluator is not involved until after the indicators have been determined. What can happen in such cases is that the design and development team might focus on the technical or academic aspects of the effort and fail to link what is being done to the goals and objectives identified by those sponsoring the effort.

As mentioned, the concepts of change and relevant indicators are an essential part of a process view of learning. We recognize that some prefer an events perspective that might be associated with moments of discovery reported by individuals. The problem with an events view, however, is that it overlooks precursor activities that lead up to a discovery moment. In Gagné's (1985) classic work entitled *The Conditions of Learning and Theory of Instruction*, he discusses five types of things to be learned (verbal information, motor skills, attitudes, intellectual skills and cognitive strategies). Gagné also recognized and emphasized the processes involved in what he called association learning, and these were later expanded to include specific cognitive processes occurring in a learner engaged in an instructional sequence. In addition, Gagné identified what he called nine events of instruction (gaining attention, identifying the learning objective, stimulating recall of prior learning, presenting what is to be learned, providing learning guidance, eliciting performance, providing feedback, assessing performance, and enhancing retention and transfer). Gagné argued that these instructional events typically occur in successful learning activities. He did not refer to those instructional events as learning events, nor did he say that they were discrete. Gagné believed that those instructional events often occurred in combinations and multiple times within an instructional sequence (see Spector, Polson & Muraida, 1993). The nine events of instruction were never intended to be a step-by-step recipe for the design of learning, as too many have misunderstood.

A second problem with an events view of learning is that it overlooks the fact that not all those involved will experience such discovery moments during instruction. Examining the entire instructional sequence and the progress of individuals over time and through instruction and experience is relevant to the intended outcomes of educational technology efforts aimed at improving learning.

A products view of an educational technology learning effort also suffers limitations. Learning as an **educational product** objectifies an effort in terms of things such as certificates, degrees, grades, graduation rates, job placements, and so on. The problem inherent in such a view is that it rarely links an instructional intervention or learning approach directly to the product. Unless there has been a controlled experimental study, it is quite difficult to link the product outcome to what preceded that outcome, and such studies are rare and difficult to conduct in actual educational settings. Moreover, the notion of change is often overlooked; when included in a product account of learning, the change typically involves a comparison with a baseline study of a group prior to the instructional intervention or new learning approach. Again, this approach can only indicate a correlation and often fails to link specific learning and instructional activities to the outcomes reported. However, efforts to design, develop and deploy educational technology products (e.g., learning applications, devices and management systems) are among the things that can and should be evaluated.

For these reasons, we proceed with a process view of learning, as such a view allows for research and evaluation, and it is especially well suited for assessing individual progress of learning over time, which is an important component of many educational technology evaluations.

Types of learning

An important distinction is that between intentional and non-intentional learning. The kind of learning typically involved in educational technology efforts is intentional, in that the learning is goal-directed, planned and purposeful. This is essential for evaluation, since a critical part of an evaluation effort of an educational technology effort aimed at improving learning will be to determine and report the extent to which those goals were met for a group of individuals. Keep in mind that in this textbook series the word 'assessment' is used to refer to individuals or groups (i.e., as assessing human knowledge and performance) whereas the word 'evaluation' is used to refer to projects, programs, products, practices and policies. Of course what is evaluated often involves human learning, so assessments will become part of an evaluation, but the focus of the evaluation is on the larger context as opposed to being focused just on individuals.

Much learning is of course non-intentional in the sense that it is not planned or purposeful and occurs incidentally or accidentally in the course of other activities. Some educators who focus on the significance of discovery moments also focus on the significance of non-intentional learning in the course of an individual's life. An example of such learning is discussed in the *Foundations* volume (Spector, 2012, 2016) involving Leo Tolstoy on a visit to Paris in the middle of the nineteenth century. Tolstoy happens upon a public execution by accident, and witnesses what he considered a barbaric and brutal execution. Tolstoy did not plan to witness the execution, nor did he intend to learn anything about French civilization. However, he records in his journal (published after his death as *Confessions*) that the event *changed* his life. He gave away his fortune; he quit writing novels aimed at fame and fortune; he took up teaching in a rural school in Russia. Those changes were seen by others and they *persisted* long after his witnessing the execution. In short, Tolstoy learned something that day that persisted years afterwards from that unplanned event.

However, to imagine that one can plan such life-changing events as part of an instructional sequence is somewhat misguided. It is misguided because planning for the occurrence of discovery moments in an instructional sequence is an example of intentional, planned learning. The fact that the goal exists in the designer's plan and is withheld from the learner (at least until after the discovery moment) does not constitute non-intentional learning. It is worth noting that pure discovery learning has not proven to be very effective, whereas guided and scaffolded discovery learning (**intentional**

learning) has shown some promise in a variety of situations (Kirschner, Sweller, & Clark, 2006).

Test Your Understanding

1. Which of the following are examples of tasks and concerns shared by instructional designers and evaluators?

   a. needs assessment
   b. problem definition
   c. requirements analysis
   d. targeted learners
   e. targeted outcomes

2. Which of the following are reliable indicators of learning having occurred?

   a. students report liking the learning experience;
   b. students complete assigned learning tasks;
   c. there is a significant improvement in what students know and can do;
   d. what students know and can do persists long after the instruction has ended; or
   e. students report liking the instructor.

Performance

Defining Performance

The word 'performance' has several uses in ordinary language that include a musical or theatrical event, a demonstration of athletic prowess, and a presentation before a group of individuals. What these uses of 'performance' have in common are observable actions or behaviors with the further implication in many cases that those actions and behaviors might serve as indicators of having attained a certain level of distinction. The use of 'performance' in this volume is consistent with popular usage, but our use places emphasis on how particular actions and behaviors indicate the attainment of targeted ability, competence, knowledge or skill. Moreover, from an evaluation perspective, it is important that the performance indicators be observable, at least indirectly, so that others can confirm or deny that a particular performance met, exceeded or failed to meet targeted outcomes.

Types of Performance

In evaluating educational technology, it is most often human performance that is the focus, but there are cases when the performance of a technology is the focus of an evaluation (e.g., how efficiently and effectively a Web-based feedback mechanism provides meaningful and informative feedback to learners). In those cases, it is still important to have observable indicators linked to targeted outcomes. In the case of an automated feedback mechanism, the performance indicators might include how quickly the feedback is provided, how accurate the feedback is, and how it leads to a successful next effort on the part of a learner, assuming such indicators comprise a significant part of the intended outcomes of the effort.

Test Your Understanding

1. Which of the following involve a performance and in what ways?

   a. replacing a memory chip in a computing device;
   b. writing an essay on the causes of poverty in a particular country;
   c. repeating Edgar Allen Poe's poem "The Raven" from memory;
   d. proving that the number π is an irrational number; or
   e. hiking the entire length of the Appalachian Trail (about 3500 kilometers).

2. Why is it important to have performance indicators?

Instruction

Defining Instruction

The word 'instruction' has a variety of uses in ordinary language. One common use is in reference to a set of steps to be followed in assembling an object or installing software. Those kinds of instruction are basically structured steps to be followed in a procedure; the assumption being that following those steps carefully will result in successful performance of the procedure. Instruction can more generally refer to a planned sequence of activities and set of associated resources intended to promote learning and improve performance. It is this latter use that is the focus of many educational technology efforts, because it is that use that provides a basis of determining the adequacy of the activities and resources in supporting the intended outcomes.

Given that context, the simple and straightforward definition of instruction is anything that is intended to facilitate, foster, support and/or enhance learning and/or improved performance. With this broad definition, a list of steps to be followed in performing a particular procedure can still be considered instruction (assuming that the intent is to support learning and not just an immediate activity to be forgotten once completed). The interest of the instructor and the evaluator are somewhat similar: to what extent did the instruction contribute to improved learning and performance. While the instructor is focused on individuals, the evaluator is focused on an entire group or population and the adequacy of the instruction in helping that group.

Learning, Performance, Instruction and Technology

As an advance organizer for the notion of a theory of change, it is worth mentioning that learning, performance and instruction can be construed in terms of enabling factors or aspects. For example, in determining the extent to which instruction is effective and efficient, one might consider the impact of the instruction on attitudes, engagement, motivation, perceived relevance or other potential enablers.

Likewise, many performances can be deconstructed into specific components. This is a common practice in coaching an athlete's performance (e.g., in golf, the enablers might include the grip, the stance, the swing, etc.).

One can also deconstruct learning into enablers. Robert M. Gagné (1968) proposed the concept of learning hierarchies as a way to organize learning activities and instructional sequences. A learning hierarchy generally proceeds from simpler learning tasks that enable a higher-order learning task based on transfer of learning from simpler tasks to more complex tasks that embed or include the simpler tasks. Joseph Scandura (1970) proposed a particular way to organize learning hierarchies in terms of lower-order and higher-order rules. Reigeluth and Stein (1983) described Elaboration Theory, which suggests a particular way to use enablers in an instructional sequence that begins with an epitomizing example. Milrad, Spector, and Davidsen (2003) refined these notions in terms of a general framework that involves graduated complexity and a sequence that leads from familiarization learning, through inquiry-based exploration to decision-making rules and policy formulation.

In short, based on theory, research and evidence from cases, an instructional planner will devise a sequence of enabling steps linking the current state of affairs to a desired state of affairs. That linkage is called a theory of change and is dealt with in more detail in Part II of this volume. For the designer, the sequence from a current state, through enabling steps and activities to a desired state will inform how the effort is structured. For the evaluator, having the entire sequence well-articulated is important. The evaluator can and should provide feedback to key persons about those links in terms of their coherence and the adequacy of the evidence in support of the links. The evaluator may also design a **fidelity of implementation** study (typically a sequence of studies comprising the major part of a formative evaluation) that provides feedback to the effort to improve links and associated efforts. Fidelity of implementation plans are discussed in Part III of this volume. The terminal parts of the enabling learning, performance and instructional sequences often form the key components of an **impact study** as those should be linked back to the original goals and objectives. Impact studies are discussed in Part IV of this volume.

Once the links from the initial state to the final state are identified, the role of technology can be considered. As it happens, there are likely to be several roles that technology can play, ranging from support technologies (e.g., an online learning management system or a student information system) to key technologies that form the basis of planned interventions (e.g., interactive augmented realities or automated feedback mechanisms for well-defined learning tasks). A particular challenge when integrating technology into learning, performance and instruction is to keep the focus on the planned learning activities and outcomes, rather than allowing the focus to shift to the specific technologies involved. The evaluator's task is to repeatedly ask how, why and in what ways a planned use of technology is likely to support attainment of the goals and objectives. Those questions should inform the effort and play a critical role in both formative and summative evaluations.

Integrative and Interdisciplinary Interventions

It should be clear at this point that planning and implementing interventions to improve an educational system or learning environment are complex activities subject to change and involving people with different backgrounds and interests. That is why the *Foundations* volume identified these six pillars of educational technology: (a) communication, (b) interaction, (c) environment, (d) culture, (e) instruction and (f) learning (see Figure 1.1; Spector 2012, 2016).

As it happens, an evaluator could structure formative evaluations or fidelity of implementation studies to include key factors from each of these areas. For example, in the area of communication, the evaluator could observe how those designing an intervention communicate with those who will deploy or use the intervention. Lack of appropriate and ongoing dialogue among planners, implementers and users can result in a suboptimal effort and disappointing results.

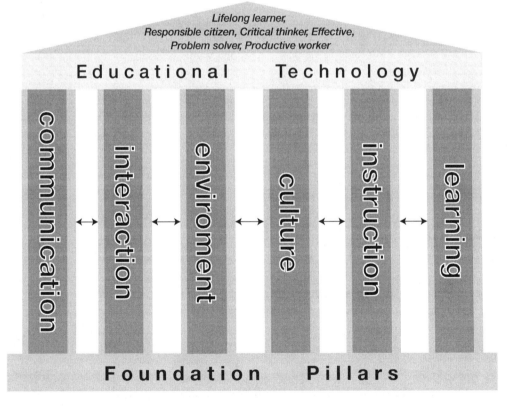

FIGURE 1.1 Foundation of Educational Technology (from Spector 2012, 2016)

Likewise, failure to take into account the culture of a primary constituency can result in the effort being perceived as offensive or not being embraced by the targeted users. Yet another example might involve an assumption on the part of designers that teachers will be able to use a new tool and teaching approach because an initial tryout of a prototype with developers yielded a positive ease-of-use finding. The possibility of overlooking significant differences in perspectives increases when actual end-users are not involved in design and development.

The point of these reminders of the complexity of educational technology is to emphasize the positive role that an evaluator can play in addressing the interdisciplinary and integrative nature of educational technology efforts. This role of facilitating cohesion, focus and collaboration across and within each of the six pillars is especially important for the evaluator just as it is important for the leaders of the effort.

An Educational Technology Evaluation Challenge

A large public university has decided to begin offering e-learning programs and MOOCs (massive, open, online courses). The first program to be involved in this five-year plan is a master's level program in educational leadership that targets K-12 school principals and school district supervisors, who will be working full-time. The first course to be offered is entitled "Integrating Technology across the Curriculum" and covers such topics as (a) cost–benefit analysis, (b) the TPACK approach to technology integration, and (c) the promises and pitfalls of technology in learning and instruction. You have been identified as the external evaluator for this effort. You cannot run and hide.

Learning Activities

1. Develop a short (no more than two double-spaced pages) white paper on educational technology evaluation for this context.
2. List 5 to 10 questions that you will ask program/project leaders in your initial discussion with them.
3. List 3 to 6 references to provide to program/project leaders to help them refine their goals and objectives.

Links

The Internal Centre for Educators' Learning Styles (ICES) has many resources pertinent to learning and instruction—see www.icels-educators-for-learning.ca/

Evaluation of the Enhancing Education through Technology Program—report to the US Department of Education developed by SRI in 2009; see www2.ed.gov/rschstat/eval/tech/netts/finalreport.pdf

A Roadmap for Education Technology—2010 report to the National Science Foundation led by Beverly Park Woolf; see www.cra.org/ccc/files/docs/groe/GROE%20Roadmap%20for%20Education%20Technology%20Final%20Report.pdf

An Introduction to the Evaluation of Learning Technologies—paper by Martin Oliver published in Educational Technology & Society in 2000; see www.ifets.info/journals/3_4/intro.html

Other Resources

The National Center for Research on Evaluation, Standards, & Student Testing (CRESST)—a well-established center to study evaluation, standards and testing at the University of California-Los Angeles; see www.cse.ucla.edu/index.php

The Theory into Practice Database—a comprehensive set of resources developed by Greg Kearsley with theories and concepts about human learning and instruction; see www.instructionaldesign.org/about.html

Educational Technology Evaluation Framework—resources developed by the University of British Columbia's Faculty of Medicine; see www.ehealth.med.ubc.ca/projects/past-projects/edtech-evaluation/

References

Blumenfeld, P. C., Soloway, E., Marx, R. W., Krajcik, J. S., Guzdial, M., & Palincsar, A. (1991). Motivating project-based learning: Sustaining the doing, supporting the learning. *Educational Psychologist, 26*(3&4), 369–398. Retrieved from www.academia.edu/2487241/Motivating_project-based_learning_Sustaining_the_doing_supporting_the_learning

CTGV (Cognition and Technology Group at Vanderbilt) (1990). Anchored instruction and its relationship to situated cognition. *Educational Researcher, 19*(6), 2–10. Retrieved from www.calteach.ucsc.edu/aboutus/documents/AnchoredInstruction.pdf

Collins, A., Brown, J. S., & Newman, S. E. (1987). *Cognitive apprenticeship: Teaching the craft of reading, writing, and mathematics* [BBN Technical Report #403]. Champaign, IL: University of Illinois at Urbana-Champaign. Retrieved from www.ideals.illinois.edu/bitstream/handle/2142/17958/ctrstread techrepv01987i00403_opt.pdf?sequence=1

Dewey, J. (1938). *Experience & education*. New York: Touchstone/Kappa Delta Pi. Retrieved from ·.ww.ruby.fgcu.edu/courses/ndemers/colloquium/experienceeducationdewey.pdf

Gagné, R. M. (1968). Learning hierarchies. *Educational Psychologist, 6*(1), 1–9.

Gagné, R. M. (1985). *The conditions of learning and theory of instruction* (4th ed.). New York: Holt, Rinehart & Winston.

Kirschner, P. A., Sweller, J., & Clark, R. E. (2006). Why minimal guidance during instruction does not work: An analysis of the failure of constructivist, discovery, problem-based, experiential, and inquiry-based teaching. *Educational Psychologist, 4*(2), 75–86. Retrieved from www.projects.ict.usc.edu/itw/vtt/Constructivism_Kirschner_Sweller_Clark_EP_06.pdf

Lave, J., & Wenger, E. (1990). *Situated learning: Legitimate peripheral participation*. Cambridge, UK: Cambridge University Press.

Milrad, M., Spector, J. M., & Davidsen, P. I. (2003). Model facilitated learning. In S. Naidu (Ed.), *Learning and teaching with technology: Principles and practices* (pp. 13–27). London: Kogan Page.

Reigeluth, C. M., & Stein, F. S. (1983). The elaboration theory of instruction. In C. M. Reigeluth (Ed.), *Instructional-design theories and models: An overview of their current status* (pp. 338–381). Hillsdale, NJ: Erlbaum.

Scandura, J. M. (1970). The role of rules in behavior: Toward an operational definition of what (rule) is learned. *Psychological Review, 77*, 516–533.

Spector, J. M. (2012). *Foundations of educational technology: Integrative approaches and interdisciplinary perspectives*. New York: Routledge.

Spector, J. M. (2016). *Foundations of educational technology: Integrative approaches and interdisciplinary perspectives* (2nd ed.). New York: Routledge.

Spector, J. M., Polson, M. C., & Muraida, D. J. (Eds.) (1993). *Automating instructional design: Concepts and issues*. Englewood Cliffs, NJ: Educational Technology.

two

Projects, Programs, Products, Practice and Policy

Education is the most powerful weapon you can use to change the world.

(Nelson Mandela, from a speech in 1993)

Given the discussion and definitions offered in Chapter 1, it is clear that a strong focus in educational technology is placed on change—more specifically, in improving a situation that is regarded as deficient or problematic in some way. It should also be clear that determining the extent to which desired changes occurred and an explanation of why observed changes did or did not occur as planned is a primary focus of evaluation.

In this chapter, the focus is on the nature of things that are developed to help bring about desired changes. Many of these things involve technology either directly (e.g., a technology-based learning activity) or indirectly (e.g., a technology-based tutorial for teachers who will implement a new educational regimen). The particular things that we have chosen to include in our educational technology evaluation framework include projects, programs, products, practice and policy. The latter two items (practice and policy) often involve technology but are seldom evaluated appropriately, which is why we have chosen to include them in this volume. More attention has been paid in the evaluation literature to projects, programs and products. Our emphasis will be on those efforts that involve technology, of course.

Change

Since the focus is on change, it is worth noting that over time some change is likely to occur regardless of what actions and decisions are taken by humans. The goal, of course, is to select actions and decisions that are likely to promoted desired changes.

When one of the authors was at the University of Bergen, he had the opportunity to work with many master's students in both Norway and Sweden in the broad area of simulation-based learning environments. He had come across a simulation environment called Beefeater Restaurants (see www.strategydynamics.com/microworlds/beefeater/; a much earlier version was used when this experience occurred), which was highly regarded in the **system dynamics** community. Basically, Beefeater put the user or a team of users in the role of managing a restaurant chain. Given decisions on a half dozen parameters (meal price, staffing payments, marketing and maintenance, menu development, and investment capital requested), the business could grow and develop into a chain of restaurants or it could lose money and go out of business. Users had the opportunity to make quarterly **inputs** based on how the restaurant was doing with the goal of staying in business for ten years and growing the restaurant chain over that time period. This author used the simulation environment to 75 graduate students in a semester length course about educational technology. Students spent several hours early in the course trying to stay in business for ten years. Only one of those 75 students managed to succeed, and that student was unable to replicate the decisions made.

This disappointing experience proved insightful for two reasons. First, the author asked the creators of the Beefeater microworld if they had similar experiences in using it with their students at the London Business School. Without hesitation they said yes. The next question was this: "Why do you use it?" The answer was simple: "Our incoming MBA students are all very bright and believe they already know everything. When they fail in the Beefeater microworld, that failure puts them in a position of wanting to understand why—to learn something." That interchange was a powerful reminder that failure can be motivating and an incentive to learn, when properly supported, of course.

The second insight occurred later when the author introduced students to Beefeater as a precursor to designing effective learning environments. In that introduction, students were shown the system and then asked to interact quarterly for ten years (in simulation time) to see what would happen if they did not change any of the six parameters. This was the *do-nothing strategy*, which worked for about five years. Not bad if you are close to retirement, but it created a need to understand the dynamics of that system. A few suggestions were then made with regard to those dynamics—namely, (a) spending more money on marketing has a delayed effect, (b) spending money on improving the menu also has a delayed effect, (c) paying staff more has a more immediate impact and may yield more customers than improving the restaurant's ambience, (d) menu price and money spent on food quality are related, and so on. Such guidelines were not all delivered at once, and only provided between simulation runs when relevant. Having small user groups discuss what happened in the previous quarter and what might be likely to happen in the next quarter proved somewhat effective in many cases, but not in all cases.

The point being made here is that education is about change. Promoting effective changes in learners is a primary goal of many efforts. Scaffolding technology-based efforts with relevant feedback from a teacher, peers, a tutor, or an automated instructional system is likely to help promote learning. Regardless of what is done to facilitate desired changes, the evaluator needs to have a thorough understanding and documentation of everything that has been done to support the effort, including tips and reminders provided informally to learners. Monitoring group discussions between simulation runs turned out to suggest that learning was occurring partly as a result of those discussions. It is not sufficient to just report that changes occurred. Explaining what contributed to those changes is important to evaluators as well as to designers.

Interventions

Given that change is pervasive, that technologies change, and that technologies change what people can and want to do, it is not surprising to find technologies associated with the changes that are sought in an educational context. After all, technology involves the practical and purposeful application of knowledge (Spector 2012, 2016), and in the case of educational technology, those applications are generally intended to contribute to the development of knowledge, understanding, skills and competencies.

An educational intervention is a planned effort to introduce a change that is likely to result in desired outcomes. The logic of an intervention might be represented as follows:

Things are not as they should be (not T).
Based on a review of the literature and other cases, if we do intervention I, then things will improve (T).
Therefore, we should do I.

The logical form of this reasoning is simple: (a) If I, then T; (b) I; (c) Therefore T. It is a compelling argument form, assuming ample evidence to support the first premise and a proper implementation of the intervention. However, an evaluator might point out that while there is some evidence that intervention I has resulted in improving T in many cases, there are significant differences between those cases and this situation. Moreover, there are other possible inventions that have been shown to have a positive influence on T.

While that kind of early feedback from an evaluator may not change the plan to proceed with a particular intervention, it is helpful to ensure that there is reasonable grounds to justify the time, effort and cost of developing and deploying intervention I. In some cases, such early feedback from an evaluator might lead the team to pursue an alternative course of action. The only downside of an evaluator questioning the evidence linking I to T or its relevance to this case is that future input from the evaluator might not be sought or it might be ignored. How an evaluator provides formative feedback is often just as important as the content of that feedback. In many cases, the feedback can be given in the form of probing questions: Is there sufficient evidence that I leads to T or that a different intervention might have a larger impact or that what was learned from other cases applies to this situation? In any case, elaborating the premise that *If I, then T* to something more specific and potentially more robust is generally desirable:

If I when P and Q, then T. Such a refined premise is likely to strengthen the justification for the intervention and help planners develop a strong theory of change (see Part III in this volume).

Test Your Understanding

1. Which of the following are subject to change during the course of developing an educational technology intervention?

   a. the level of funding for the effort;
   b. the personnel involved in design, developing and deploying the effort;
   c. the capabilities of the technologies selected to support the effort;
   d. leadership of the institution supporting or hosting the effort; or
   e. the goals and objectives of the effort.

2. In addition to change, what other important characteristics are a critical concern with regard to educational technology efforts to improve learning and instruction?

Projects

A project is a planned effort to bring about desired outcomes that has a budget, resources, a definite beginning, a duration, and reasonably well-defined goals and objectives. Examples of educational technology projects include such things as the introduction of MOOCs in a university's offerings, the integration of social networking in an online learning course, the development of automated feedback mechanisms that are dynamically customized to an individual's performance and preferences, and so on.

It is quite common to find evaluators involved in funded educational technology projects, as many funding agencies require that either an internal or external examiner be identified and an evaluation plan submitted as part of the project proposal. A representative example of the requirement of a funding agency to include emphasis on evaluation is the American National Science Foundation's STEM+ Computing Partnerships (STEM+C) program (see www.nsf.gov/pubs/2015/nsf15537/nsf15537.htm).

Some funding agencies require both an internal evaluator (or evaluation team) and an external evaluator (or evaluation team), especially for large, multi-year efforts. In these cases, the internal evaluator is paid by the project whereas the external evaluator is paid by the funding agency. The primary function of the internal evaluator is to provide formative evaluation feedback as the project evolves with the goal of helping the project succeed. The primary function of the external evaluator is to provide an independent summative evaluation at the end of the effort analyzing and reporting the extent to which the project in fact succeeded. Separating formative and summative evaluation in this way (an internal evaluator for formative evaluation and an external evaluator for summative evaluation) sounds reasonable and may yield meaningful results. However, because the internal evaluator is linked directly to the effort, the ongoing formative feedback provided might not be as objective and as unbiased as would be desired. In addition, because the external evaluator has not been directly involved and integrated into the effort as it evolved, there is a challenge in explaining the degree to which the effort succeeded. In some cases, both internal and external evaluators are involved in formative and summative evaluations and may even work as one team.

The European Commission typically uses external evaluators who are not linked to nor paid by the project for large multi-year, multi-institutional educational efforts. The Commission selects several external evaluators and pays them directly to provide ongoing formative evaluation during the project and a summative evaluation at the end of the effort. The projects are also expected to have their own internal evaluation plans and evaluators who provide ongoing input and suggestions during the effort. This strategy is likely to result in detailed and robust formative and summative evaluations, but significant resources are then required, both by the project and by the funding agency.

Our view is that evaluations, both formative and summative, are critical components of a project (or other educational technology effort). Neither should be overlooked or

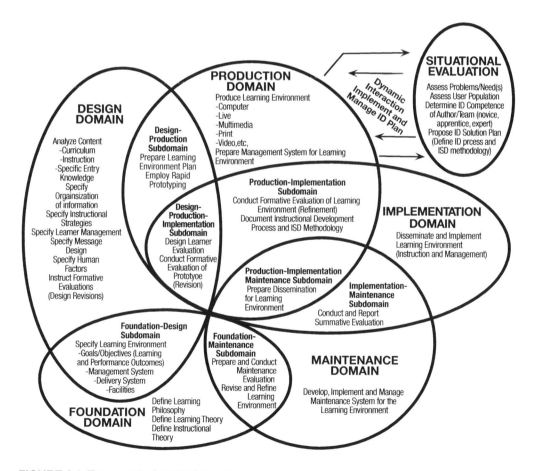

FIGURE 2.1 Tennyson's (1995) ISD-4 Model (used with permission; also appears in Spector 2012, 2016)

under-supported. One way to conceive of the role of evaluating educational technology projects is in terms of Tennyson's (1995) fourth generation ISD model (see Figure 2.1).

The two-dimensional representation of ISD-4 does not do full justice to Tennyson's (1995) description of what instructional designers and developers actually do. In particular, *situational evaluation* applies to each and all of the other clustered (domain, in Tennyson's model) activities depicted. Moreover, as Tennyson's model suggests, there are overlapping activities and concerns among the various clustered domains, and those overlapping areas should be considered priority evaluation targets. Regardless of where the effort is in terms of maturity (design, production, implementation, maintenance, etc.), a situational evaluation should be conducted to ensure that the activities associated with the domain clusters are being conducted as planned and in a reliable manner. An evaluator can contribute to those ongoing situational evaluations, either in concert with project evaluation personnel or as an additional perspective from someone not directly involved in everyday project activities.

Many of the elaborations and examples found in this volume refer to educational technology projects because many published evaluations focus on projects, largely due to the requirements of funding agencies and the need to publish findings that can move the discipline forward. The framework and strategies and methods mentioned with regard to projects apply in large part to programs, products, practices and policies, with obvious adjustments being made pertinent to the thing being evaluated and the context involved.

Programs

A program is a planned effort with high-level goals that has (or had) a definite beginning and is expected to continue, possibly with changes and refinements, for an indefinite period of time. An obvious example of an educational technology program is a university degree program with a focus on instructional design and technology. Many examples of university programs in the area of educational technology can be found (see Spector, 2015).

Another kind of educational technology program is the implementation of a particular approach involving educational technology. For example, in an effort to reform a curriculum, a decision might be made to implement a programmatic effort to embrace technology integration principles associated with TPACK (technological, pedagogical and content knowledge; see Mishra & Koehler, 2006). Still another example is the adoption of a particular technology (e.g., a learning management system) and associated practices with the intention of continuing that technology for an indefinite period of time.

Programs can be evaluated in a manner similar to that described for projects with several notable exceptions. First of all, programs typically have less well-defined goals and objectives than projects. One way that an evaluator can help in early program development is to recommend specific outcomes that are measureable and that can be associated with the overarching aims of the effort.

A second difference between projects and programs is that programs seldom have a predefined end date; programs are expected to continue indefinitely or at least as long as outcomes are acceptable. Due to the fact that the duration of a program may be much longer than that of a project, it is often necessary to revisit the situation and circumstances that motivated the introduction of the program. Are the conditions now the same as those that motivated the change to a new program? Are the assumptions still valid? Has the situation changed sufficiently to revisit the structure and organization of the program? Such questions are best answered by someone who is not directly involved in the program, such as an independent or outside evaluator. When conducting such an evaluation, questions that the sponsoring institution or agency might want answered include (a) what changes to the existing program might be desirable and how might they be implemented, (b) is there an alternative program that might be developed that is more pertinent to the current situation, and (c) should this program be continued or terminated? Because jobs and livelihoods are at stake, it seems best to ask for an outside perspective from an unbiased expert.

Test Your Understanding

1. Which of the following characteristics apply to both projects and programs?

   a. a definite start date
   b. a definite end date
   c. goals
   d. a requirement for external evaluation
   e. a need to maintain the status quo

2. The definite advantages of having an internal evaluator include:

   a. familiarity with the effort;
   b. knowledge of the context and people involved;
   c. the ability to conduct an unbiased evaluation;
   d. having external resources available to pay for an internal evaluator; and
   e. having a credible person offer critical but constructive feedback.

3. The definite advantages of having an external evaluator include:

   a. having an outsider conduct an independent summative evaluation;
   b. having a recognized outside expert offer critical but constructive feedback on a daily basis;
   c. having an independent and unbiased person analyze and report findings;
   d. having external funding sources pay for the evaluation; and
   e. having a person unfamiliar with local practices and preferences offer unbiased feedback.

Products

An educational product is a designed artifact that is intended to improve learning, performance and/or instruction. Examples of educational technology products include (a) a mobile application to teach a foreign language, (b) an online tutorial about creating tables in a word processor, or (c) an Internet-based tool that accepts a student's input (e.g., a request to identify the key factors in a complex and ill-structured problem) and then provides automated feedback pertinent to that student's input (e.g., part of an expert's response not found in the student's response). There are thousands of examples of educational technology products that one can find on the Internet. Finding products that actually contribute to improved learning, performance and instruction is a challenge.

Educational products are designed for a purpose. Sometimes the purpose is clear and specific, but not always. One task for the evaluator of an educational technology product is to determine to what extent it satisfies its intended purpose. As it happens, many products are used in ways not anticipated by the designer or developer (Norman, 1988). While it is important to ensure that an educational technology product satisfies its intended purpose, it is also important to determine how the product is being used in ways not envisioned by designers, and whether and to what extent those uses contribute to improved learning, understanding and performance. An evaluation that examines the full range of uses of and perceptions about an educational technology product is then able to recommend changes in the product or changes in how people are being trained to use the product.

One example of unintended use leading to a better next-generation product involved a product developed in a military research laboratory to help novice instructional personnel develop technology-based training programs for a variety of technical tasks (e.g., troubleshooting electronic equipment). The tool was an instructional design advising system that was example-based; it was called GAIDA for Guided Approach to Instructional Design Advising. Examples consisted of lessons that had been demonstrated independently to develop the intended knowledge and competencies. As the persons being trained in instructional design worked through an example, they could switch from student mode to designer mode and see the designer's rationale for that particular unit of instruction or activity. The system also had a note-taking capability that allowed the trainee to make notes that could then become part of a lesson design or specification the trainee would be assigned upon graduation from the course. Since the trainees were all subject matter experts and their assignments were known in advance, they began actually developing their lesson designs while doing the training. When this was discovered, a few simple changes in the software allowed the notes feature to become a lesson design specification for an actual product. That change made the learning directly relevant to the job and added motivation, engagement and empowerment to the learning experienced that had been somewhat deficient. A keen evaluation eye can help improve products as well as helping efforts succeed.

Practices

An **educational practice** refers to a set of established activities or procedures that are normally or regularly carried out in association with an educational task. An example of an educational technology practice might include a standard process for conducting a needs assessment and using a survey of relevant personnel to prioritize problems and create a requirements specification for a planned educational technology effort. A more general example of an educational technology practice is having students develop electronic portfolios, upload those to a common Website, supporting a peer review process using a standard rubric, and then using the outcomes of the peer review to determine a grade. Yet another example of an educational technology practice involves conducting a classroom evaluation visit using a notebook computer with a standard evaluation form linked to the Internet.

Educational practices are many and varied, and they make use of technologies in a wide variety of ways. Like the other things that can be evaluated, however, educational practices have a purpose. The evaluation should then be linked to the purpose of the practice. In many cases, an evaluator will find that the actual use is not well aligned with the stated purpose. For example, the stated purpose may be to improve the quality of teaching, but the actual use might be perceived as punitive (i.e., so-called problem teachers are identified and put on probation or fired). In such a case, collecting and analyzing the perceptions of all those involved is important. Identifying differences in perceived use and benefits among different groups is important and should be made known to all involved if there is a genuine desire to improve the situation (this is a basic assumption in nearly all evaluations, by the way).

It is clear that evaluators have principles and values that include ethical obligations (for example, see www.eval.org/p/cm/ld/fid=51 and www.aes.asn.au/images/stories/files/membership/AES_Guidelines_web.pdf). Some obligations are obvious, such as not releasing or disseminating confidential information. Cases involving personalities and the jobs of professionals are particular challenging. It might happen, for example, that a school principal has a view of a practice that is quite different from that of a teacher. The evaluator may have gained the information about the teacher from an interview or survey or focus group. Should the principal ask which teacher expressed the divergent view, the evaluator should respect the right of the teacher to remain anonymous (the default assumption; an exception can occur in rare cases involving agreements signed in advance). Ethical obligations will be discussed in more detail in Part IV of this volume. A good topic for discussion in class or in an online forum is the kinds of ethical dilemmas and decisions that might arise in the course of conducting evaluations.

Policy

An **educational policy** typically involves a set of mandated activities, procedures, regulations or standards that govern the conduct of various educational tasks. Policies are often closely related to practices. For example, some universities have a set of policies governing the conduct of faculty and students. In various departments there might then be procedures (the practice associated with the policy) that indicate how that department will implement a particular university policy. One task that evaluators are occasionally asked to do is to determine the degree to which departmental procedures and guidelines are aligned with university policy.

There are policies that pertain to educational technology. An example is a policy pertaining to the use of personal handheld devices in the classroom. Some schools ban such personal devices in the classroom based on the belief that they only serve to distract students. Other schools embrace the use of personal devices (BYOD, which stands for bring your own device) based on the belief that they can be used to broaden student engagement with a variety of content and enhance student learning. This example emphasizes that a policy has a purpose, like the other things being evaluated. When the purpose is clearly stated, it is possible for an evaluator to collect and analyze evidence that shows to what extent the purpose is fulfilled or the rationale justified. With regard to this BYOD issue, the evaluator might find that both policies (one for and one against BYOD) go beyond available evidence and are based primarily on opinion. When an evaluator digs into the evidence, it might happen that sometimes BYOD is helpful and sometimes not helpful, or that some teachers favor BYOD while others object, or that some students much prefer to use their own devices while others have none to use. Once such evidence is collected and analyzed by an evaluator, a more robust policy might be developed that indicates when and where and how personal devices might be used as well as how teachers might be trained in their use and how students without a device can be supported through a school-provided device. In short, an evaluator can help in the development of realistic and robust policies. Unfortunately, that rarely happens.

Test Your Understanding

1. Which of the following is an educational technology product?

   a. a Web app to play solitaire on a mobile device;
   b. a Web app to learn basic Spanish;
   c. a smart watch that alerts the wearer to incoming email;
   d. a slide rule; or
   e. a pen with a built-in digital camera.

2. How are educational technology practices and policies related? Give one example to illustrate your response.

A Representative Educational Technology Challenge

A large public university has decided to begin offering e-learning programs and MOOCs. The first program to be involved in this five-year plan is a master's level program in educational leadership that targets K-12 school principals and school district supervisors, who will be working full time. The first course to be offered is entitled "Integrating Technology across the Curriculum" and covers such topics as (a) cost–benefit analysis, (b) the TPACK approach to technology integration, and (c) the promises and pitfalls of technology in learning and instruction. You have been identified as the external evaluator for this effort. How would you proceed?

Learning Activities

1. Determine whether this effort is a project, program, product, practice or policy, or any combination of those, and indicate what aspects of the effort led to your determination.
2. Indicate what roles an internal evaluator might play in this effort.
3. Indicate what roles an external evaluator might play in this effort.
4. What might an evaluator do that would constitute early formative evaluation and feedback?
5. What might an evaluator do that would constitute a summative evaluation?

Links

The American Evaluation Association Mission, Vision, Values, and Governing Policies—see www.eval.org/p/cm/ld/fid–13

The Australian Evaluation Society—see www.aes.asn.au/join-the-aes/membership-ethical-guidelines/7-aes-codes-of-behaviour-ethics.html

Other Resources

Strategy Dynamics microworlds—see www.strategydynamics.com/microworlds/

References

Mishra, P., & Koehler, M. J. (2006). Technological pedagogical content knowledge: A framework for teacher knowledge. *Teacher College Record, 108*(6), 1017–1054.

Norman, D. A. (1988). *The design of everyday things.* New York: Basic Books.

Spector, J. M. (2012). *Foundations of educational technology: Integrative approaches and interdisciplinary perspectives.* New York: Routledge.

Spector, J. M. (2015, April). The changing nature of educational technology programs. *Educational Technology, 55*(2), 19–25.

Spector, J. M. (2016). *Foundations of educational technology: Integrative approaches and interdisciplinary perspectives* (2nd ed.). New York: Routledge.

Tennyson, R. D. (1995). Instructional systems development: The fourth generation. In Tennyson, R. D. & Barron, A. (Eds.), *Automating instructional design: Computer-based development and delivery tools* (pp. 33–78). New York: Springer.

three
Evaluation Goals and Scope

*It is good to have an end to the journey; but it is the journey
that matters, in the end.*

(attributed to Ernest Hemingway)

Evaluation is a complex and challenging activity, as strongly suggested in the opening chapters of this volume. There are many dimensions involved in evaluating educational technologies, including (a) the type of thing to be evaluated; (b) the type of evaluation being done; (c) the purpose, focus and scope of the evaluation; (d) the methods and instruments involved; (e) the types of data and information to be collected and analyzed; and (f) sensitive issues such as ethical concerns, personnel matters, language and cultural considerations, and so on. Fundamentally, evaluation is a purposeful, goal driven enterprise that is aimed at improving an effort and determining the extent the effort achieved its intended aims. Goals can be considered a starting point in developing an evaluation plan for an effort.

In addition to goals, a second important aspect of evaluation pertains to scope. In an instructional context, there are many interacting factors that influence what happens in education and training. Within the scope of an effort, there are *mediating factors* or variables (e.g., those that explain the relationships between variables) and *moderating factors* or variables (e.g., those that influence the strength of relationships between variables) (see Baron & Kenny, 1986). In addition to these variables, there are assumptions that influence the selection and development of interventions; these assumptions should be made explicit as they may change as the effort evolves. Moreover, there are factors external to the effort that can unexpectedly come to bear on the effort. Making the scope of an effort clear along with relevant assumptions will aid evaluators in helping the effort to succeed, determining the extent to which the effort succeeded, and explaining the level of success attained.

For example, an effort in a school might be aimed at the goal of improving student test scores over a five-year period relative to an average for comparable schools. An intervention is designed, developed and deployed in the first two years of the effort while baseline data is being collected. At the end of year two, there is a sudden and unexpected influx of non-native speakers from a region that experienced a massive earthquake, destroying thousands of homes in that region. These students arrive with poor language skills and no student records. In year three, test scores dropped dramatically in that school and remained low in year four. The unstated assumption was that the number and type of students enrolling in the school would remain relatively constant. That assumption was not stated since enrollments had been stable for many years. An evaluator who is intimately familiar with the school and that particular effort can explain the drop in test scores due to the influx of students independently of the deployment of the intervention.

It is important for evaluation purposes to make the scope of an effort well defined, the assumptions explicit, and factors likely to influence outcomes clear. Not everything can be controlled within the scope of an effort. Identifying factors that influence outcomes in an educational context is particularly difficult, as there are many factors and many of those factors are difficult to isolate, describe and evaluate. Just as educational research is rarely conclusive and generalizable to a wide variety of situations, the findings of an evaluation are at best probabilistic and suggestive of what and how to improve an effort or to what extent the effort succeeded. Figure 3.1 depicts the general evaluation framework adopted for purposes of discussion and elaboration in this volume.

An effort in general is intended to take things from an initial state to or towards a desired state, as depicted in Figure 3.1. It is rare to find a strictly linear or straightforward path from the starting state to the desired state, which is one of the factors that makes educational research and evaluation complex. Those involved in the effort as well as the evaluator should be asking two important questions along the way: (1) Are the planned things being done? and (2) Are those things being done well? Both of those questions guide a formative evaluation that is intended to help the effort succeed.

As depicted in Figure 3.1, there are many things to be considered in developing evaluation plans. In order to develop evaluation plans (e.g., a fidelity of implementation study and an impact study), it is important to be specific about what kinds of things will be evaluated. In many cases involving programs and projects, there are also particular products, practices and policies to take into consideration. Depending on the purpose, scope and focus of the effort and the kinds of things being evaluated, a decision can be made about which kinds of evaluators will be needed for different kinds of evaluation. Once those decisions have been made, the methods, protocols, instruments and data to be collected and analyzed can be identified. All those decisions and plans are subject to important local issues, such as the organizational culture, ethical considerations, and personnel involved.

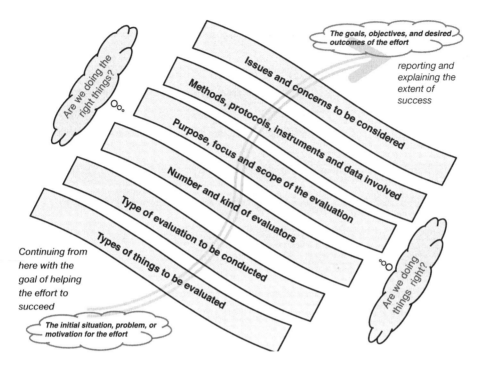

Text inside figure:
- The goals, objectives, and desired outcomes of the effort
- reporting and explaining the extent of success
- Are we doing the right things?
- Issues and concerns to be considered
- Methods, protocols, instruments and data involved
- Purpose, focus and scope of the evaluation
- Number and kind of evaluators
- Type of evaluation to be conducted
- Types of things to be evaluated
- Continuing from here with the goal of helping the effort to succeed
- Are we doing things right?
- The initial situation, problem, or motivation for the effort

FIGURE 3.1 A General Framework for Educational Technology Evaluation

Because the goals and scope of an effort are critical in formulating evaluation plans, these critical aspects of an effort are discussed next.

Test Your Understanding

1. Consider the relationship of work status (unemployed, working part time, working full time) and attrition rates in online courses. If the data collected about level of education (not a high school graduate, high school graduate but no college courses completed, less than two years of college, less than four years of college, more than four years of college) suggest that full-time workers with some college education have a lower attrition rate than others, would level of education be a mediating or a moderating variable? Why?

2. Consider the case of developing a MOOC for a new course on the history of Scandinavia between the Viking era (roughly 790 to 1066 AD) as part of an undergraduate degree program in history. The MOOC includes links to Internet sources as well as interactive quizzes based on information gathered from following the links and completing reading assignments. After existing for a year and being offered to four different cohorts of students, an evaluation is planned to determine whether the MOOC is worth continuing. Would you say this is a formative or a summative evaluation and what would you identify as the key factors to be considered?

Goals

As previously discussed, a common factor among the various things and efforts to be evaluated in an educational technology effort is a purpose or goal. Having an explicit goal for the effort is a necessity for evaluation purposes. Having a clear goal that can be operationalized in terms of observable outcomes is highly desirable, but may not exist in some cases (e.g., a large-scale government program aiming at developing a more competitive workforce may not be easily operationalized as it may be difficult to specify what a more competitive workforce is or how it is to be determined).

A task for an evaluator early in the process is, therefore, to seek clarification with regard to the goal, purpose or overall aim. If the evaluator is not involved early in the effort, this task may be delayed until a final summative evaluation study is conducted. In such a case, the evaluator has to assume the goal is whatever was stated in the initial documentation of the effort or subsequently modified in documentation that the evaluator is given. Not having an evaluator involved throughout an effort means that the evaluator cannot perform the task of helping the effort succeed.

When the goal is connected to the design, development and deployment of an effort, it is important to ensure alignment between an analysis of the initial situation, what is planned and why, and what is actually accomplished. Just as the educational technology effort is goal driven, so is the evaluation of that effort (the primary goal being to help the effort succeed with a secondary goal of reporting and explaining the extent to which it did succeed).

In many cases, there is a problem situation that is being addressed by the effort, such as declining graduation rates, low test scores, poor performance on certification exams, and so on. Such aspects of a situation might be regarded as symptoms of an underlying problem, but they also can form the basis for targeted outcomes (e.g., increase graduation rates to 95 percent within two years, or improve test scores to above average in comparison with a larger population within three years, etc.). It is not unreasonable to regard aspects of the situation that are being addressed by a particular educational technology effort to inform the desired outcomes and goals of the effort.

However, knowing the goals should not lead one directly to a solution approach. Experienced designers and educators are likely to look into probable causes and underlying reasons behind the problematic situation. For example, if the presenting symptom is a high drop-out rate or low pass rate in a particular course, the underlying causes might be related to the instructor, to the structure of the course, to how the course is related to other courses, and so on. Prior to developing a solution approach, a needs assessment or requirements analysis (see Part II for more details) might be needed in order to identify those factors that are linked to the high attrition rate or low pass rate. An evaluator who is involved early in the effort can then see that the effort is addressing the question of whether or not the right things are being done. Knowing the goal is but a first step. It is then important to understand why that goal is being addressed in a particular way and whether or not the intended activities and developments can reasonably be linked to improving the problem situation.

Understanding the goals, the motivation for the goals, and the likely factors linked to attaining the goals are all important for an evaluator. By clarifying the goals, the evaluator also helps an effort define its focus and scope, which are discussed next.

Scope

The scope of an educational technology project involves developing a clear focus based on the goals and objectives. In the process of focusing the effort, the things that are expected to have the most influence on achieving the goals need to be identified; this is a first step in helping an effort come to grips with the scope. Of all the things that can influence attainment of the goals, those that are subject to manipulation need to be identified. An educational technology effort cannot be expected to change the socioeconomic status of a learner (at least not in the short term), even though that status might have a strong correlation with student performance. There are things that influence the situation that can be addressed, and those factors are the ones that should be within the scope and focus of the effort.

For example, suppose that the problem situation is that college students are performing poorly in a required humanities course. While science and engineering majors do not perform quite as well as others, the difference is not significant. Moreover, in the most problematic part of the course involving seventeenth century art, all majors are performing poorly. After conducting interviews with students along with a survey, the instructor identifies lack of motivation as the underlying problem, and, as a consequence is looking for ways to improve motivation for that unit of instruction. A designer is consulted who believes that the structure of the seventeenth century art unit is not done well and that the assessment involved aims only at a simple memory task of matching a painting with an artist. The designer probes further and asks the instructor what knowledge and skill the students typically lack that should be developed in that particular unit of instructor. The instructor says it would be nice if students could link a picture of the painting entitled *A Naval Encounter between Dutch and Spanish Warships* with the artist Cornelis Verbeeck. The designer asks "Why?" The instructor answers that it would demonstrate some knowledge of seventeenth century Dutch artwork. Further discussion reveals that students are expected to be familiar with 100 paintings and their artists by the end of that unit of instruction that lasts for three weeks.

The designer does some outside work examining the content and methods used in the course and returns to the instructor with the following suggestion:

> Would a student who could explain the differences among the depicted warships in terms of ship construction knowledge at that time reflect some pertinent know-ledge? Or, would a student who could discuss the historical context of the depicted sea battle be demonstrating pertinent knowledge? How about a student who knew the history of that particular painting and how it was cut in half and later restored?

After much discussion, the instructor comes around to the view that memorizing 100 paintings and their artists has very little practical value for anyone other than an art historian. The instructor further admits to wanting students to become art historians, although that has happened to only two students in the last 20 years of that instructor's experience. The designer then poses a different approach linked to a motivating activity with small groups of students studying a small number of paintings and developing a portfolio for each one that includes the historical context, a short biography of the artist, and details of the painting that are innovative or especially creative.

The point of this extended example, which is based on an actual case, is that an evaluator who is part of the effort from the beginning will have access to the instructor, the designer and perhaps also to a representative sample of students. Having detailed knowledge of how the effort evolves from the initial problem situation is important in developing evaluation plans. In this example case, once the new approach is resolved, the evaluation will focus on how well that approach is implemented. Sometimes it takes more than one try to get the new approach right. In any case, after determining that the effort is doing the right things, the evaluator will look to see whether things are being done well. Are the groups being formed effectively? Do groups have access to the proper resources? Is there adequate time to develop the art portfolios?

Once the evaluator has determined that the right things are being done and that they are being done in a satisfactory manner, then the evaluator is in a position to examine outcomes and determine to what extent the effort succeeded and explain why. Ideally, the formative evaluation (Are the right things being done and are they being done right?) and the summative evaluation (To what extent and why did the effort succeed?) are linked and ideally performed by the same evaluator or evaluation team. We realize that this rarely happens, but it is a preferred and comprehensive evaluation approach.

In the course of observing and documenting how a solution approach emerges and is modified, the focus and scope of an effort should become very clear. One responsibility of an evaluator is to help the effort specify the focus and scope, which coincides with what an instructional designer may be doing for the project. While the designer's perspective is on what technologies to use to achieve an effective and efficient solution, the evaluator's perspective is on understanding why particular technologies can be expected to work and how well they in fact work in terms of achieving desired outcomes.

To conclude this chapter on goals and scope, it is worth remarking that some educational technology programs include an emphasis on both design and evaluation, although that dual emphasis is all too rare. The more common occurrence in educational technology programs is to emphasize design and development (Spector, 2015).

Test Your Understanding

1. Explain the relationships that exist among the context, scope and goals of an effort, including an elaboration of the implications for evaluation.

A Representative Educational Technology Challenge

Extending the previous educational technology challenges, again consider a large public university that has decided to offer e-learning programs and MOOCs. The first program to be involved in this five-year plan is a master's level program in educational leadership that targets K-12 school principals and school district supervisors, who will be working full-time. The first course to be offered is entitled "Integrating Technology across the Curriculum" and covers such topics as (a) cost-benefit analysis, (b) the TPACK approach to technology integration, and (c) the promises and pitfalls of technology in learning and instruction. You have been identified as the external evaluator for this effort. How would you start planning formative and summative evaluations for this effort?

Learning Activities

1. In your own words, develop what you believe would be reasonably considered as the goals, scope and focus of the effort (for the challenge project or an effort of your choosing).
2. What kinds of things would you consider to answer the following two questions as the effort evolves: (a) Are the right things being done? and (b) Are things being done right?
3. What would you identify as the outcome variables to form the basis of a determination of the degree to which the effort succeeded?

Links

European Commission evaluation guidelines published in 2006—see www.ec.europa.eu/europeaid/evaluation/methodology/examples/guide3_en.pdf

OECD evaluation guidelines developed by the Austrian Development Cooperation in 2009—see www.oecd.org/development/evaluation/dcdndep/47069197.pdf

University of Michigan guidelines for evaluating teachers—see www.crlt.umich.edu/tstrategies/guidelines

UK Research Council evaluation guidelines—see www.rcuk.ac.uk/Publications/policy/Evaluation/

Other Resources

The Learning Development Institute is dedicated to human learning and has developed extensive resources freely available to the public. Of particular relevance is *The Book of Problems*—see the list of resources for 2002 at www.learndev.org/

An Introduction to the Evaluation of Learning Technology—paper by Martin Oliver available at www.ifets.info/journals/3_4/intro.html

Institute of Museum and Library Services Website for evaluation resources—see www.imls.gov/research/evaluation_resources.aspx

US Office of Educational Assessment Website with evaluation links—see www.washington.edu/oea/resources/program_eval.html

US Centers for Disease Control Website with many links to evaluation resources—see www.cdc.gov/eval/resources/

Canada's International Development Research Centre Website with evaluation methods and resources—see www.idrc.ca/EN/Programs/Evaluation/Pages/PublicationsList.aspx

International Consortium for the Advancement of Academic Publications Website with a rich collection of resources and methods for social science research—see www.gsociology.icaap.org/methods/

References

Baron, R. M., & Kenny, D. A. (1986). The moderator–mediator variable distinction in social psychological research: Conceptual, strategic, and statistical considerations. *Journal of Personality and Social Psychology, 51,* 1173–1182.

Spector, J. M. (2015). The changing nature of educational technology programs. *Educational Technology, 55*(2), 19–25.

four
Types of Evaluations

Everything that can be counted does not necessarily count;
everything that counts cannot necessarily be counted.
                                        (attributed to Albert Einstein)

Once goals and objectives have been clarified and the scope and focus of the effort clarified, the appropriate type of evaluation can be determined. In some cases, a sponsoring agency or institution will dictate that an independent evaluation team should conduct a summative evaluation at the end of the effort or at a predetermined time in a program. In other cases, the evaluation is left to those organizing the effort. Ideally, there will be both a formative evaluation and a summative evaluation. The former is conducted periodically in an ongoing manner and is aimed at helping the effort to achieve the best possible outcomes. The latter is conducted at the end of the effort (or at a predetermined point in the case of ongoing programs) and is aimed at reporting the extent to which the effort has succeeded and explaining why.

In addition to formative and summative evaluations, evaluations can also be categorized as being internal (conducted within the resources of the effort and as an integral part of the effort) or external (conducted by an independent evaluator or team with resources typically provided by the funding agency).

Another way to characterize the types of evaluations is by what is being evaluated and at what level. As previously mentioned, project evaluations are the type most often reported in the literature, primarily because funding agencies require evaluation for funded efforts. Program evaluations are also common, especially when large-scale or prestigious programs are involved. Product evaluations are often reported as alpha and beta tests and commonly associated with software and digital devices. It is less common to find evaluation of practices reported in the literature, but these should not be neglected as they can contribute significantly to the understanding of what educational technologies work, when, in which circumstances and why. Policy evaluations typically occur in reaction to an apparent failure of an existing policy, and these are not widely reported with regard to educational technology policies, unfortunately. A recent example, however, concerns policies governing the use of social networking and smartphones in the classroom, as these have drawn the attention of parents and the general public.

Finally, evaluations can be conducted by individuals or by teams. The larger the effort, the more likely it is to have an evaluation team involved. Each of these types of evaluation is discussed briefly in the remainder of this chapter.

Evaluation Targets

The targets of educational technology are most often projects and programs, but software and hardware products as well as practices and policies related to educational technology are sometimes evaluated. A common evaluation framework is one developed by Donald Kirkpatrick in 1959 that contains four levels of evaluation, as noted in Table 4.1.

In identifying the target of an evaluation, it is important to keep in mind the larger context, including the instructional objectives and learning outcomes. Gagné and Merrill (1990) argued that a typical learning task involves a set of integrated knowledge and specific skills, which they called an *enterprise*. Examples of an enterprise include such things as replacing the radar unit in an aircraft, developing a budget plan for a project

Table 4.1 Kirkpatrick's four levels of evaluation

Kirkpatrick's Level	Evaluation Focus
Reaction	What participants thought and felt about the instruction; overall satisfaction with regard to the value, relevance and quality of the experience from the learner's perspective are typically elicited on simple evaluation forms at the conclusion of the instruction.
Learning	What learners gained in terms of knowledge, skills and attitudes; this level typically involves tests and observations of performance administered during and at the end of the instructional sequence.
Behavior	What knowledge, skills and attitudes are transferable from the instructional environment to the work or everyday situation; this level of evaluation typically occurs some time after the instruction ends (e.g., 3 to 6 months), and it is typically accomplished by observation and testing.
Results	What the impact of the instruction has had as a consequence of the instruction, typically from an organizational perspective in terms of improved quality or productivity of the individual's performance on the job, although this could also involve an individual or societal perspective (e.g., selection of career, advancement, etc.).

or designing a flotation device to raise sunken objects to the surface of a body of water. While it might be appropriate to teach parts of an enterprise in the course of an instructional sequence, what matters in terms of the learner developing the desired knowledge and skill is best determined by the learner's understanding of and performance with regard to the targeted enterprise. This notion is consistent with van Merriënboer's (1997) notion of targeting whole tasks of increasing complexity as a learner progresses through an instructional sequence. Identifying miscues in the performance of an enterprise or whole task is useful in helping a struggling learner make progress (**formative assessment**) as well as in helping to improve the instruction to reduce the occurrence of such miscues (formative evaluation).

Table 4.2 indicates the typical concerns associated with various targets of an educational technology evaluation. Note that the concerns for projects and programs are similar, as are the concerns for practices and policy. The reasons for those similarities and relevant differences make a good topic for a classroom or online discussion.

By no means are the representative concerns in Table 4.2 comprehensive or exhaustive. The intention is only to suggest that the focus of an evaluation should be adjusted to fit the kind of thing being evaluated. Elaborations of evaluation plans for the different types of things to be evaluated are provided in Part IV of this book. An in-class or online discussion activity could be to elicit examples of each type of educational technology being evaluated and discuss the major concerns for that case. There are additional concerns discussed below that are a function of the level of the effort and whether the specific evaluation is formative or summative.

Table 4.2 Evaluation targets and associated concerns

Target Type	Representative Evaluation Concerns
Projects	Alignment with goals and objectives; fidelity of implementation; timeliness and quality of planning and implementation; impact on intended outcomes; appropriate training and support; sustainability and maintainability; satisfaction and use
Programs	Alignment with goals and objectives; impact on intended outcomes; unintended outcomes; sustainability and maintainability; adequacy and availability of resources required for continuation
Products	Alignment with goals and objectives; suitability, usability, scalability, sustainability, learnability and affordability; level of adoption; user satisfaction; contribution to quality and productivity
Practice	Alignment with goals and policies; adequacy of training; levels of awareness, adoption and adherence; contribution to achieving goals; appropriate degrees of flexibility and autonomous decision making; existence of feedback and monitoring mechanisms
Policy	Alignment with goals; levels of awareness, adoption and adherence; contribution to achieving goals; appropriate degrees of flexibility and autonomous decision making; need for policy adjustments

Scope and Level

Table 4.3 represents the notion that the scope and level of the evaluation have an impact on the structure and substance of the evaluation. For the purpose here, we simplify the issue by focusing only on the level, as that is a major factor in determining the scope of an effort. For example, if the level is a single course, then the scope is reasonably limited to that course and perhaps comparison courses. If the level is institutional, however, then a variety of courses are likely to be involved, or perhaps all courses at the institution. Moreover, an evaluation focused at one level might require or include evaluations conducted at another level.

It is not uncommon to have things at a lower level in Table 4.3 included as part of the evaluation for something at a higher level. For example, at the program level, the major concerns of a summative evaluation might be an analysis of trends in the last five years with regard to completion times and rates. Since a program might involve a number of courses, an analysis might be conducted at the course level to determine pass rates as that might have an impact on program completion rates. In a similar manner, when evaluating a course with regard to grades, it is reasonable to examine performance in specific modules and lessons as that can affect grades in a course.

Test Your Understanding

1. State the four levels of evaluation in Kirkpatrick's model, and briefly indicate the purpose of the evaluation at that level.
2. Identify typical evaluation concerns for an evaluation at the project level.
3. Identify typical evaluation concerns for an evaluation at the practice level.

Formative Evaluations

A **formative evaluation** is conducted during an effort to help ensure that the effort succeeds or achieves the best possible outcomes. A **formative assessment** of a student

Table 4.3 Evaluation scope and representative concerns

Evaluation Scope or Level	Representative Evaluation Concerns
Global/National	Cultural, economic, political factors
Institutional	Mission, ratings, performance criteria
Program	Effectiveness, graduation rates, job placements
Curriculum	Professional requirements, competencies
Course	Requirements, objectives, pass rates, grades
Module/Unit	Coherence, sequencing, context, satisfaction
Lesson	Objectives-assessments linkage, content–objectives linkage
Activity	Feedback, rubrics, linkage to objectives, cumulative understanding

(or group of students) is aimed at identifying gaps in a student's knowledge and performance so that those gaps can be directly addressed and remediated, with the goal of improving that student's performance or understanding. Parallel to formative assessments of students are formative evaluations of various things (projects, programs, products, practices and policies), each of which is a designed entity that can potentially be improved. The fundamental notion is that which is designed can usually be designed better. With regard to things intended to support learning, the general goal is design or re-design the targeted thing so as to achieve improved learning outcomes. In order to improve something, it is important to know how well it is currently working. As a consequence, with regard to educational technologies, formative assessments of students (and teachers and tutors and others who support learning) using those technologies or affected in some way by those technologies are often relevant.

In addition to examining the influence on students, teachers or technical personnel, a formative evaluation will often look at how well the thing has been designed or re-designed and how adequate the training and support associated with the development and adoption of the technology has been. In short, there are five areas of focus in a formative evaluation that can be represented in the form of questions: (1) Does the design fit the indicated problems and goals? (2) How well is the design being implemented? (3) How adequate is the training and support for the effort? (4) How closely are those involved in the implementation following guidance and procedures provided? (5) What problems have been identified that have not been (or cannot be) addressed, and what is their likely effect on outcomes?

A conceptual framework for implementation fidelity typically includes the nature of the problem or situation involved, the kind of intervention planned and its justification, required support and maintenance, training of relevant personnel, quality issues, responsiveness of participants, measurements, and likely moderators (Carroll et al., 2007). Of relevance to a fidelity of implementation plan in the context of a formative evaluation is an explanation of how an undesirable or problematic situation will be transformed into a more desirable state of affairs; that explanation is often called a theory of change (more details are available in Part II). The specific activities and actions that are part and parcel of the theory of change become the focus of a formative evaluation or fidelity of implementation study. As a consequence, it is frequently the case that a fidelity of implementation study will include both quantitative and qualitative data. An elaborated fidelity of implementation plan is included in Part III and an example provided in Part IV.

Summative Evaluations

A summative evaluation is conducted at the end of effort (or at a predetermined point in time for an ongoing program) to report the extent to which the effort succeeded along with an explanation of why that level of achievement occurred. It is often the case that an independent evaluation by an outside expert or team of experts is asked to perform a summative evaluation. A summative evaluation should be directly linked to the goals and objectives identified at the initiation of the effort. In a sense, the effort is being held accountable to those goals and objectives, and the summative evaluation is the basis for that accountability. Broadly speaking, a summative evaluation is an impact study. The fundamental question is this: What impact, if any, did the effort have on targeted outcomes? Because the goals and objectives should lead to measureable or observable outcomes, a summative impact study is relatively straightforward to construct. In many cases, quantitative methods are involved, although a comprehensive summative evaluation will link back to a formative evaluation study and often include a qualitative component to explain why a particular level of success occurred.

Nearly every funded project has to design, conduct and report the findings of an impact study. As it happens, such a study is often publishable in the form of educational research in the refereed academic literature. Funding agencies generally encourage and support such publications in the form of research findings as the results of a well-conducted summative evaluation can contribute to the educational technology knowledge base with regard to what works, when and why. In short, the evaluation of an educational technology effort constitutes a recognized form of educational technology research. Moreover, regardless of whether or not the findings report significant outcomes, a summative evaluation in the form of an impact study can inform future practice and policy development, especially when coupled with a rich and robust fidelity of implementation study.

Test Your Understanding

1. Explain why a tight coupling of formative and summative evaluation is generally desirable.

Internal and External Evaluations

Another consideration with regard to evaluation is who will be planning, implementing and analyzing the findings of the evaluation. Will it be one person or a team of individuals? Will the evaluator or evaluation team be part of the implementation and effort and funded with the budget of the effort? Or will the evaluator(s) be external to and independent of the effort in terms of funding and reporting responsibility? Will the evaluator(s) plan, implement and analyze findings or will that be accomplished by different persons with different reporting responsibilities?

There is no single evaluation approach or standard answer to these questions. Evaluation practices vary from effort to effort, from agency to agency, and from place to place. An evaluation plan may be written by the effort's principal investigator prior to there being an evaluator involved. When that happens, a more detailed evaluation plan is often developed once an evaluator is involved in the effort.

We have suggested that it is very beneficial to have a tight connection between the formative and summative evaluation, and that is obviously more likely when the same individual or team is involved. When the evaluator or evaluation team is external to and independent from the effort, it is more challenging for the evaluator(s) to gain deep insight into the actual conduct of the effort; what is gained in terms of independence may be lost in terms of specificity and granularity of the evaluation (especially the formative evaluation). The cost–benefit tradeoffs of external vs. internal evaluators is difficult to determine. As a result, many agencies develop a standard for evaluations. A common standard is to require the project to have one or more evaluators and conduct periodic internal formative evaluations and report those as well as a summative evaluation to the project leader as well as to the funding agency. With large-scale, multi-year efforts it is more likely that an external evaluation team will be involved in both formative and summative evaluations. That is in fact how the European Commission often structures evaluations for the networks of excellence that it funds, for example.

Individual and Team Evaluations

It was mentioned in the previous section that there may be one person doing the evaluation or it might be a team of individuals. Moreover, the design, implementation and analysis of findings may be done by different persons or teams, although that is somewhat unusual and can introduce confusion and discontinuity. In general, the larger the effort in terms of institutions and people involved, funding support, and length of time involved, the more likely it is that there will be a team of evaluators. The size of the evaluation team can vary, but it is usually 3 to 5 persons. The expertise and specializations required for a full and fair evaluation influence who should be part of an evaluation team. With large efforts involving an evaluation team, it is generally desirable to have an expert in the domain of application, an expert in methodology and data analysis, and an expert in the particular technologies involved.

A Representative Educational Technology Challenge

Continuing with the previous case of a large public university that has decided to offer e-learning programs and MOOCs, the first program to be involved in this five-year plan is a master's level program in educational leadership that targets K-12 school principals and school district supervisors, who will be working full time. The first course to be offered is entitled "Integrating Technology across the Curriculum" and covers such topics as (a) cost–benefit analysis, (b) the TPACK approach to technology integration, and (c) the promises and pitfalls of technology in learning and instruction. What do you think are the key factors influencing the success of this effort and how are they related?

Learning Activities

1. Identify the typical concerns associated and indicate at what level for the above effort.
2. Indicate whether you would recommend an internal or external evaluator and why.
3. Identify the particular aspects of the effort on which you would focus in a formative evaluation.

4. Identify the particular aspects of the effort on which you would focus in a summative evaluation.

Links

infoDEV Website for Knowledge Map: Impact of ICTs on Learning and Achievement—see www.infodev.org/infodev-files/resource/InfodevDocuments_154.pdf

The Institute of Education Sciences Website entitled "Logic Models: A Tool for Designing and Monitoring Program Evaluations" by Biran Lawton, Paul Brandon, Louis Cicchinellil, and Wendy Kekahio—an excellent source for an overview of program evaluation located at www.ies.ed.gov/ncee/edlabs/regions/pacific/pdf/REL_2014007.pdf

The National Science Foundation Grant Proposal Guidelines, which contain guidelines for the research and evaluation plans associated with an effort—see www.nsf.gov/pubs/policydocs/pappguide/nsf15001/gpg_index.jsp

The Association for Educational Communications and Technology (AECT) Website has extensive resources for instructors and the use of technology to support instruction—www.aect.org

The American Society for Training and Development (ASTD) Website has extensive resources for professional trainers—www.astd.org/

The International Society for Performance Improvement (ISPI) Website has extensive resources pertaining to training and performance improvement—www.ispi.org/

Other Resources

The Institute of Education Sciences at the US Department of Education What Works Clearinghouse is a good source for the kinds of evidence that can support research and evaluation—see www.ies.ed.gov/ncee/wwc/default.aspx

The National Center on Evaluation, Standards, & Student Testing at UCLA has many articles, assessments, rubrics, games, games, guidebooks, reports and other resources pertaining to evaluation and assessment—see www.cse.ucla.edu/

The American Institutes for Research Website for Program and Policy Evaluation in Education is especially useful for broad evaluations involving large-scale programs and policies—see www.air.org/page/program-and-policy-evaluation-education

The Center on Response to Intervention of the American Institutes for Research has a number of resources on implementation and evaluation, focused on response to intervention, of course—see www.rti4success.org/related-rti-topics/implementation-evaluation

Wested.org Website with many free publications on research and evaluation—see www.wested.org/resources/product-category/highlights/research/#

The SRI International Website on Educational Impact Evaluation has many relevant resources for evaluation and assessment—see www.sri.com/research-development/impact-evaluation

References

Carroll, C., Patterson, M., Wood, S., Booth, A., Rick, J., & Balain, S. (2007). A conceptual framework for implementation fidelity. *Implementation Science, 2*(1), 40–49.Retrieved from www.implementationscience.com/content/pdf/1748-5908-2-40.pdf

Gagné, R. M., & Merrill, M. D. (1990). Integrative goals for instructional design. *Educational Technology Research and Development, 38*(1), 23–30.

Kirkpatrick, D. L. (1959). Techniques for evaluating training programs. *Journal of the American Society of Training Directors, 13*(3), 21–26.

van Merriënboer, J. J. G. (1997). *Training complex cognitive skills: A four-component instructional design model for technical training*. Englewood Cliffs, NJ: Educational Technology Publications.

five

Major Evaluation Tasks

True genius resides in the capacity for evaluation of uncertain, hazardous, and conflicting information.
(Sir Winston Churchill)

Tennyson's fourth generation instructional systems design model (see Figure 2.1) highlights the close relationship that exists between design, development and evaluation. In Tennyson's model, there is a situational evaluation component for nearly every design and development activity, especially for critical points as the design, production, implementation, and maintenance of an effort progresses. According to Spector, Polson & Muraida (1993), evaluation of the kind that Tennyson encapsulated in Figure 2.1 can be categorized into these primary categories: (a) quality evaluation, (b) internal evaluations (a.k.a, alpha tests), (c) field evaluations (a.k.a. beta tests), and (d) after-implementation tests. In the evaluation literature, the first three of these generally comprise a formative evaluation with the fourth being the key concern of a summative evaluation (or a formative evaluation when there are anticipated cycles of major periodic reviews and revisions, as is the case with many software products) (Bates, 2004; Greene, Caracelli, & Graham, 1989; Lynn, 2014).

In light of the situation motivating an educational technology effort and the goals and objectives of that effort, there are many tasks to be accomplished to transform a current situation into a more desirable situation (see Figure 3.1). Evaluators can be and should be involved in any of the associated processes and activities in Tennyson's model (Figure 2.1) asking questions pertaining to the quality of a particular activity, whether or not that activity is doing the right things, and to what extent those things are contributing to the desired outcomes. Answering those questions can be part of a formal evaluation or an informal evaluation, each of which is described next.

Informal Evaluations

There are many occasions when those involved in planning and implementing an educational effort will ask an evaluator or someone with evaluation knowledge and experience, especially with regard to educational technologies, to take a look at a specific aspect of the effort and give feedback with regard to possible improvements. Such an instance is an example of what Tennyson called situational evaluation and is often done as a kind of quality review. If these quality reviews are not a planned part of a formal evaluation with a prescribed structure and protocol, they constitute a kind of informal evaluation. Other instances occur spontaneously as a particular aspect of the effort emerges for consideration and a second opinion as to its relevance and likely significance in the context of the effort is sought. An informal evaluation is one that occurs more or less when needed or desired and outside the context of a planned formative or summative evaluation. A well planned formative evaluation will include many focused evaluations as an effort progresses, but the reality is that having very targeted quality reviews conducted on an ad hoc basis can help keep an effort moving forward and minimize problems later.

When asked to perform an informal evaluation, quality check or quick review, it is important to have the goals and objectives clearly in mind. It is also important to understand what assumptions have been made by the planners as well as what unexpected events or circumstances might occur over the life of the effort that could invalidate assumptions or change the direction, goals and objectives of the effort. The advantage of having an evaluator perform informal quality reviews is that an evaluator is likely to have or develop a clear context for the effort, whereas having a colleague selected for the sake of convenience might lead to a much more narrow informal evaluation. The point we are emphasizing here is that a serious effort to ensure the success of the effort is important. An informal evaluation is a kind of formative evaluation and should not be overlooked as a way to help achieve desired outcomes.

Formal Evaluations

Formal evaluations are those that are planned and designed. There are two general types: formative and summative. Each type of formal evaluation should have an associated evaluation plan. Evaluation plans are normally constructed in the context of the effort, with formative evaluation plans focused on the planning, development and implementation of the effort and summative evaluation plans focused on the intended outcomes and impact of the effort.

One kind of study associated with a formative evaluation is a fidelity of implementation study, which will be described in more detail in a subsequent chapter. A fidelity of implementation study is a systematic determination of the alignment of the goals and objectives with what is being developed and implemented. The focus is not merely on the features of a particular technology or approach but also includes the context needed for the effort to succeed, which often involves training and professional development for teachers, administrators and support personnel. The questions that drive a fidelity of implementation study are: (a) Is the effort evolving as planned? (b) Are the right things being done and are they being done well?

An impact study is a common form of summative evaluation. A typical impact study will be directly linked back to the goals and objectives of the effort. Goals are often stated in terms of broad and often vague long-term, medium-term and short-term aims. The latter are more easily operationalized in terms of observable measures and become the primary focus of an impact study. For example, the problematic situation of an effort could be that college graduation rates in engineering are lower than desired. The short-term goal of the effort is to improve graduation rates for engineering majors (perhaps by 10 percent within two years). The reason low graduation rates in engineering is a problem is that many engineering jobs go unfilled and companies are falling behind in terms of productivity and global competitiveness. That means a medium-term goal could be to place more graduates in engineering jobs to improve workforce productivity. A longer-term goal might be to make the state more competitive in the engineering sector of the economy. The medium- and long-term goals are not easily operationalized and require a longer period of time to measure that might be beyond the scope of a particular effort. The rationale for long-term goals is important, as it makes assumptions and other aspects of the situation explicit. However, it is usually the short-term outcomes of the effort that link directly back to specific goals that form the basis of an impact study. In the case of longitudinal studies that cover longer time periods, a summative evaluation would include medium-term outcomes and perhaps long-term outcomes as well as short-term outcomes.

What Evaluators Do

Given the kinds of evaluations with which evaluators can be involved, and the variety of things accomplished in an educational technology effort, evaluators are often asked to do many things. Table 5.1 indicates many of the tasks evaluators do along with the associated context for that task; this is not an exhaustive list, nor is it meant to provide relevant details of the activities and responsibilities associated with a particular task.

A good topic for discussion in class or in an online forum are other tasks that evaluators might be or have been asked to do.

In closing this chapter, we want to emphasize that there is a close connection between evaluation and design, which is most obvious through activities described above in the categories of informal evaluation and formative evaluation (see also Black & Wiliam, 1998; Schröter, Maura, & Coryn, 2015; Smith, 2008).

Table 5.1 Evaluation tasks and responsibilities

Evaluation Task	Task Content
Help write and edit a proposal	Contribute to the proposal prior to the initiation and funding of an effort
Draft and refine evaluation plans	Contribute detailed evaluation plans to a proposal and edit the proposal from an evaluation perspective
Perform an informal quality check	Respond to the requests for ad hoc feedback on specific aspects of the effort
Conduct a fidelity of implementation study	Develop, validate and implement methods, instruments and protocols
Analyze and report results of an implementation study	Formative evaluation report provided to the leadership (and sponsors) of the effort
Advise leadership of the effort as it evolves	Provide ongoing advice as requested or when deemed important to
Conduct and report results of an impact study	Summative evaluation report to leadership and sponsors of the effort

Test Your Understanding

1. What broad questions might guide a fidelity of implementation study?
2. What specific questions might be part of a fidelity of implementation study?
3. Are informal evaluations typically considered formative or summative in nature? Why?

A Representative Educational Technology Challenge

Continuing with the previous educational technology challenges, again consider a large public university that has decided to offer e-learning programs and MOOCs so as to reach working adults unable to take time off for full-time residential studies. The first program to be involved in this five-year plan is a master's level program in educational leadership that targets K-12 school principals and school district supervisors, who will be working full time. The first course to be offered is entitled "Integrating Technology across the Curriculum" and covers such topics as (a) cost–benefit analysis, (b) the TPACK approach to technology integration, and (c) the promises and pitfalls of technology in learning and instruction. You have been identified as the external evaluator for this effort, and you lead a small three-person evaluation team. You have been asked to develop plans for both formative and summative evaluations of this effort. The effort is still in the early planning stages. How might you organize the evaluation plans?

Learning Activities

1. Identify the various tasks that your team should undertake during this effort.
2. Describe the kinds of things that would be relevant to a formative evaluation of the effort.
3. Describe the kinds of things that would be relevant to a summative evaluation of the effort.
4. What would you advise the effort's leader with regard to the type, frequency and value of informal evaluations as the effort evolves?

Links

SRI's Online Evaluation Resource Library (OERL), with the support of the USA National Science Foundation, has a rich collection of very high quality resources—see www.oerl.sri.com/

Learning Resources Evaluation Guidelines prepared by the Saskatchewan Ministry of Education—see www.education.gov.sk.ca/learning-resource-evaluation-guidelines

The USA National Science Foundation Evaluation Center (EvaluATE) focused on advanced technological education—see www.evalu-ate.org/

Other Resources

The Higher Education Academy Open Educational Resources infoKit—see www.openeducationalresources. pbworks.com/w/page/62697426/OER-Evaluation

The Department of Education of Prince Edward Island's Evaluation and Selection of Learning Resources: A Guide—see www.gov.pe.ca/photos/original/ed_ESLR_08.pdf

The USA Department of Education's Fund for the Improvement of Secondary Education (FIPSE) evaluation requirements, guidelines, and resources—see www2.ed.gov/about/offices/list/ope/fipse/evaluate.html

The USA Governmental Accountability Office (GAO) publication on Designing Evaluations: 2012 Revision —see www.gao.gov/assets/590/588146.pdf

The University of Washington's Office of Educational Assessment Website with program evaluation resources—see www.washington.edu/oea/resources/program_eval.html

Elsevier's Studies in Educational Evaluation journal—see www.journals.elsevier.com/studies-in-educational-evaluation/

Elsevier's Evaluation and Program Planning journal—see www.journals.elsevier.com/evaluation-and-program-planning/

Springer's Educational Assessment, Evaluation and Accountability journal—see www.springer.com/education+%26+language/journal/11092

Sage's Educational Evaluation and Policy Analysis journal—see www.epa.sagepub.com/

Taylor & Francis/Routledge's Educational Research and Evaluation journal—see www.tandfonline.com/toc/nere20/current

Practical Assessment, Research & Evaluation, the independent, open, online journal—see www.pareonline.net/

NOAA Office of Education and Sustainable Development paper on Designing Evaluation for Education Projects—see www.wateroutreach.uwex.edu/use/documents/NOAAEvalmanualFINAL.pdf

References

Bates, R. (2004). A critical analysis of evaluation practice: The Kirkpatrick model and the principle of beneficence. *Evaluation and Program Planning, 27*(3), 341–347.

Black, P., & Wiliam, D. (1998). Assessment and classroom learning. *Assessment in Education: Principles, Policy & Practice, 5*(1), 7–71.

Greene, J. C., Caracelli, V. J., & Graham, W. F. (1989). Toward a conceptual framework for mixed-methods evaluation designs. *Educational Evaluation and Policy Analysis, 11*(3), 255–274.

Lynn, G. (2014). Revising an engineering design rubric: A case study illustrating principles and practices to ensure technical quality of rubrics. Practical Assessment, Research & Evaluation, 19(8). Retrieved from www.pareonline.net/getvn.asp?v=19&n=8

Schröter, D. C., Magura, S., & Coryn, C. (2015). Deconstructing evidence-based practice: Progress and ambiguities. *Evaluation and Program Planning, 48*(1), 90–91.

Smith, C. D. (2008). Design focused evaluation. *Assessment & Evaluation in Higher Education, 33*(6), 631–645.

Spector, J. M., Polson, M. C., & Muraida, D. J. (Eds.) (1993). *Automating instructional design: Concepts and issues.* Englewood Cliffs, NJ: Educational Technology.

part two

AN EVALUATION
FRAMEWORK

six

Needs Assessment

Understanding human needs is half the job of meeting them.

(Adlai Stephenson, 1952)

A project has a goal and objectives, a beginning and an ending. The beginning could be a needs assessment. A needs assessment is an important part of program/project development and evaluation. It provides vital information for the development of project goals, objectives and answers to the questions: what is, what should be, and what needs are the most critical? This chapter presents a discussion for the planning and implementing of a needs assessment. While a step-by-step model is presented to guide assessments, the planning process should be viewed as dynamic and flexible, able to be tailored to the specific organizational and environmental characteristics of the projects.

Examples of Needs Assessment

- A school district seeks community consensus on the implementation of a *bring your own device* (BYOD) policy to allow students to use personally owned devices in school.
- The e-learning task force of a university collects data to examine the pedagogical needs of using flipped classrooms.
- A library system of a city investigates the information needs of the community, both its patrons and potential library users.
- A primary school conducts a needs assessment to determine how best to meet the diverse learning needs of students in implementing blended learning.

These examples are only a few of the many types of needs assessment that are conducted for a variety of purposes. The following sections provide a background on needs assessment and introduce a three-phase model for conducting a needs assessment.

Background on Needs Assessment

Why Conduct a Needs Assessment?

In general, when there is a need for something, that thing would presumably improve a situation or a desired outcome cannot happen without satisfying the need. Among the many uses of the term 'need', Witkin and Altschuld (1995) suggest that 'need' as a noun, on the one hand, refers to the gap or discrepancy between a present state (what is) and a desired end state, future state, or condition (what should or could be). The need is neither the present nor the future state; it is the gap between them. On the other hand, 'need' as a verb points to what is required or desired to fill the discrepancy—as in a solution or a means to the desired end state. There is an important difference between needs and solutions. McKillip (1998) suggests that the use of the term 'need' may involve instrumentality and moral concern. The instrumental nature of a need statement consists in a factual assertion of a means–ends relationship. Instrumental need statements suggest but do not impel action, for such needs are open to empirical investigation and verification. A sense of moral concern often is attached to a need statement and can guide or compel action.

Do we already know what we need? Obviously, the answer to this question is not a definite yes or no. There is plenty of information from the press, media, and reports on indicators of needs in education, business, industry, government, etc. However, a needs assessment is conducted to collect evidence and derive information and perceptions that will benefit specific groups of people. A needs assessment is not intended to provide diagnostic information about individuals; rather it offers a useful and rational approach to identifying and describing specific areas of need, discovering factors contributing to perpetuation of needs, and devising criteria for plans to meet or ameliorate the need (Witkin and Altschuld, 1995).

Needs Assessment and Needs Analysis

There are different terms used to depict the process of identifying and describing needs and areas of need. For example, Watkins and Kaufman (1996) differentiate needs assessment from needs analysis: "Needs assessment identifies the gaps in results and thus provides the basis for deriving useful and justifiable objectives. Needs analysis identifies what causes the needs and then identifies the solution requirements" (Watkins & Kaufman, 1996, p. 12). Whereas McKillip (1998) suggests needs analysis is a decision-aiding tool used for resource allocation, program planning, and program development in the fields of health, education, and human services, and it has two primary components: "need identification and need assessment. For need identification, information is gathered on those in need, their environments, problems confronting them, and solutions to these problems. For need assessment, this information is synthesized, ordering options for the originating decision" (p. 261). Some writers used the terms needs assessment and needs analysis interchangeably (Benjamin, 1989).

Needs assessment should be focused on particular target groups in a system. A system is a set of regularly interacting elements that form a unified whole organized for a common purpose. An important characteristic of a system is that the parts are interdependent. Anything that affects one part of the system typically has consequences for other parts and the whole system. Common target groups in education settings include students, parents, teachers, administrators, and the community at-large. Witkin and Altschuld (1995) further explain needs assessment in terms of three levels of needs, each of which represents a target group for the needs assessment (Table 6.1).

First, needs assessments are initially conducted to determine the needs of the people (i.e., service receivers) for whom the organization or system exists, and students are examples in education settings. However, a comprehensive needs assessment often takes into account needs identified in other parts of a system. For example, a needs assessment might include the concerns of the service providers (e.g. teachers, guidance counselors, or school principals—the people who have a direct relationship with the service receivers) or, at a different level, system issues (e.g., availability of programs, services and personnel; level of program coordination; and access to appropriate facilities).

Needs Assessment

In this chapter, needs assessment is defined as "a systematic set of procedures undertaken for the purpose of setting priorities and making decisions about program or organizational improvement and resource allocation. The priorities are based on identified needs" (Witkin and Altschuld, 1995, p. 4). Needs assessment focuses on the ends (i.e., outcomes) to be attained, rather than the means (i.e., process). For example, academic achievement is an outcome whereas teacher instruction is a means toward that end. It gathers data by means of established procedures and methods designed for specific purposes. The kinds and scope of methods are selected to fit the purposes and context of the needs

TABLE 6.1 Levels of needs and target groups

Levels of Needs	Target Groups	Examples
Level 1	Service receivers	Students, clients, patients, information users, customers
Level 2	Service providers and policymakers	Teachers, parents, social workers, caretakers, health care professionals, librarians, managers, administrators
Level 3	Resources or solutions	Facilities, buildings, equipment, supplies, technology, programs, class size, surgical procedures, work conditions

assessment. Needs assessment sets priorities and determines criteria for solutions so that managers and administrators can make sound decisions. It sets criteria for determining how best to position and allocate available resources, people and facilities. Finally, needs assessment leads to action that will improve programs, services, organizational structure and operations, or a combination of these elements (OME, 2001).

Test Your Understanding

Which of the following is an example of the target group for needs assessment in Level 1?

a. teachers
b. time allocations
c. commuters
d. program delivery system

Which of the following is an example of the target group for needs assessment in Level 2?

a. transportation
b. school supervisors
c. patients
d. salaries and benefits

A Three-Phase Model of Needs Assessment

Many types of organizations, such as governmental agencies, school systems, social service agencies, corporations, hospitals and universities, conduct needs assessments to guide and inform decision making. A three-phase model of needs assessment is proposed by Witkin and Altschuld (1995). Table 6.2 shows a general plan for assessing needs in three phases with a time progression for a given set of tasks. However, the boundaries between these phases are not fixed.

Phase 1: Pre-assessment

As an exploration, Phase 1 aims (a) to investigate what is already known about the needs of the target group, (b) to determine the focus and scope of the needs assessment, and (c) to gain commitment for all stages of the assessment, including the use of the findings for program planning and implementation. The output of Phase 1 is a preliminary plan for Phase 2 to conduct the main assessment. Common tasks for Phase 1 include the following (OME, 2001):

TASK 1: Prepare Management Plan
- The project manager or evaluator is the key person who will be responsible for the planning and management of the assessment, and will ensure the success of the project under one's leadership.

TABLE 6.2 Three-phase needs assessment model

Phase 1 Pre-assessment (exploration)	Phase 2 Assessment (data gathering)	Phase 3 Post-assessment (utilization)
• Prepare a management plan	• Determine context, scope, and target groups	• Set priorities on needs
• Identify major issues	• Gather data to define needs	• Consider possible solutions
• Determine measures and indicators	• Prioritize needs	• Evaluate and select solutions
• Consider data sources and methods	• Analyze and identify causes	• Propose action plan
• Decide preliminary priorities	• Summarize findings	• Communicate results
Output	**Output**	**Output**
Preliminary plan for phase 2	Criteria for action based on high-priority needs	Action plan, written and oral briefings, and reports

- Form a Needs Assessment Committee (planning group). The members of a Needs Assessment Committee should be the representatives of the organizations and/or individuals that are critical to ensuring commitment and follow-up actions.
- Determine a schedule for reporting to the senior management team and other important stakeholders in time. It is critical to discuss major issues with senior team members over a certain period of time.

TASK 2: Identify Major Issues
- Reach consensus on the goals (desired outcomes) of greatest importance to the target group.
- Refine the list of goals to the top 3 to 5 goals.
- Brainstorm a list of concerns/issues for each goal.
- Decide on the major concerns/issues for each goal.

TASK 3: Determine Measures and Indicators
- Identify measures and indicators that are data that could verify the concerns/issues exist.

TASK 4: Consider Data Sources and Methods
- Determine what kinds of information would be helpful to more clearly define the need and where and how to collect the data.

TASK 5: Decide Preliminary Priorities
- Set the priorities of each concern/issue and attach great importance to those priorities during the data collection.

Test Your Understanding

Which of the following are major functions of Phase 1?

    a. to collect data;

    b. to form a planning committee;

    c. to consider possible solutions; or

    d. to identify measures and indicators.

Phase 2: Main Assessment

The task of the Phase 2 is to document the status of concerns and issues, to compare the status with the vision of desired outcomes or end states, and determine the magnitude of the needs and underlying causes (OME, 2001). The major output from this phase is a set of needs statements in tentative order of priority based on the criticality of the need and its causes.

TASK 1: Determine Context, Scope, and Target Groups
- Determine the scope of the needs assessment—e.g., all students in the BYOD project.
- Determine target groups—e.g., students in the BYOD project, parents, teachers, etc.

TASK 2: Gather Data to Define Needs
- Specify a desired outcome based on the goals of the program.
- Collect data to determine the current state of the target group in relation to the desired outcome.
- Formulate need statements based on discrepancies between current and desired outcomes.

TASK 3: Prioritize Needs
- List concerns/issues (need areas) in rank order of importance (e.g., school network system, teaching resource).
- Within each area of concerns/issues, separately rank the identified needs (e.g., teacher-student contact, peer network).

TASK 4: Analyze and Identify Causes
- Determine general and specific causes of high priority needs. Try to answer the question "Why does this need persist?"
- Analyze and identify the factors that are amenable to intervention with control of your program.

TASK 5: Summarize Findings
- Summarize and document findings by need with an explanation of the major causes.

- Share the results with the Needs Assessment Committee, managers and other key stakeholders.

Test Your Understanding

Which of the following are major functions of Phase 2?

a. to gather data;
b. to form a planning committee;
c. to consider possible solutions;
d. to analyze and identify causes.

Phase 3: Post-assessment

Phase 3 is the bridge from the analysis to actions—to use needs assessment findings to plan to attain desired outcomes (OME, 2001). It answers these important questions: What needs are the most critical? What are some possible solutions? Which solutions are best? The output of Phase 3 includes an action plan along with written and oral briefings and reports.

TASK 1: Set Priority on Needs
- Criteria for assigning priorities among needs are based on several factors:

    - the magnitude of discrepancies between current and target states;
    - causes and contributing factors to the needs;
    - the degree of difficulty in addressing the needs;
    - risk assessment—the consequences of ignoring the needs;
    - the effect on other parts of the system or other needs if a specific need is or is not met;
    - the cost of implementing solutions; and
    - other factors that might influence the effort to meet the need.

- Set priorities in two stages: (a) broad areas, such as goals, concerns/issues (needs) or target groups; and (b) critical needs within each area.

TASK 2: Consider Possible Solutions
- Set criteria (or standards) for judging the merits of alternative solution strategies. At a minimum, proposed solutions should meet the criteria of effect on causes, acceptability, and feasibility (includes resources).
- Generate and examine potential solutions. In examining possible solutions—review and document research and evaluation data that supports the merits of each alternative.

TASK 3: Evaluate and Select Solutions
- Evaluate and rate each solution separately against the evaluation criteria.

- Consider whether each of the high-ranking solutions will drive toward the contemplated change or whether they will end up in the opposite direction and prevent change.
- Based on all the collected information, select one or more solutions for each need area.

TASK 4: Propose Action Plan
- The plan should include descriptions of the solutions, rationale, proposed timelines and resource requirements.

TASK 5: Communicate Results
- At the end of this phase, a written report should be prepared to communicate the methods and results of the needs assessment to decision makers, policymakers and key stakeholders.
- The report should include:
  - description of the needs assessment process;
  - major outcomes (identified needs);
  - priority needs (and criteria used to determine such priorities);
  - action plan (with the data and criteria used to arrive at the solution strategies); and
  - recommendations for future needs assessments.

Test Your Understanding

Which of the following are major functions of Phase 3?

a. to propose an action plan;
b. to form a planning committee;
c. to consider possible solutions; or
d. to identify measures and indicators.

Key Factors in Conducting Needs Assessment

Both planners and evaluators conduct needs assessments, but often from different viewpoints and in different contexts. In planning, needs assessment is the essential first step in documenting needs and developing programs or other strategies to meet them. The major job of evaluators is to decide the extent to which a program/project has been successful in meeting its goals. Evaluators also conduct needs assessments to identify goals, problems or conditions that should be addressed in future program/project planning. Needs assessments may be conducted in an iterative planning-evaluation cycle (Witkin & Altschuld, 1995). The key factors in conducting needs assessment are summarized as follows (OME, 2001):

- The active use of a Needs Assessment Committee is one important method for obtaining expert advice and gaining commitment to the process and using the results.
- Make sure needs focus on desired outcomes and are listed as the gaps between "what is" and "what should be."
- Before you gather data, spend the time to investigate what is known about the needs of the target group—to identify all of the concerns.
- Develop measurable need indicators to guide your data collection process.
- Perform a causal analysis—Ask "why" does this need still exist? To solve a problem, planners must understand it first.
- Share information with decision makers, policymakers, and stakeholders throughout the needs assessment process. Frequent communication with these groups is important for the "buy in" needed to use the needs assessment results.
- Document the research base for potential solutions.
- Prepare a written report that describes the methods and results of the needs assessment.
- Finally, there is no one perfect needs assessment model or procedure since the needs assessment is a dynamic and flexible process.

Learning Activities

A cluster of 12 special schools in a city, serving students with different kinds of special needs, conduct a needs assessment to determine the development of an e-learning platform to meet the learning diversity of students, to give teachers flexible access to information and pedagogical resources, and to help the principals to manage their schools. If you were asked to conduct such a needs assessment, how would you proceed?

Given the scenario above, follow the appropriate TASKs in the three-phase model and describe:

- how you will identify the problem(s) involved, the causes, whether the resulting needs are instructional in nature, and the possible solutions;
- what technique(s) you will use to collect data and how you will analyze the data. Write a brief paragraph on your data collection techniques and analysis procedures;
- what information sources you will use. Identify the people, documents, and metrics you will consult; and
- how you will use and present the results of your needs analysis? Write one or two sentences to describe how and to whom you will report your results.

Links

Methods for Conducting an Educational Needs Assessment—see www.cals.uidaho.edu/edcomm/pdf/BUL/BUL0870.pdf

Guide to conduct a comprehensive needs assessment of your community—see www.ovcttac.gov/taResources/OVCTAGuides/ConductingNeedsAssessment/pfv.html

Needs Assessment Strategies for Community Groups and Organizations—see www.extension.iastate.edu/communities/assess

Coordination Tools: Needs Assessment—see www.unocha.org/what-we-do/coordination-tools/needs-assessment

Other Resources

Complete Resource Site on Needs and Needs Assessments; see www.needsassessment.org/

References

Benjamin, S. (1989). A closer look at needs analysis and needs assessment: Whatever happened to the systems approach? *Nonprofit Management Leadership, 28,* 12–16.

McKillip, J. (1998). Need analysis: Process and techniques. In L. Bickman & D.J. Rog (Eds.) (1998). *Handbook of applied social research methods* (pp. 261–284). Thousand Oaks, CA: Sage.

OME (2001). *Comprehensive needs assessment.* Retrieved from www2.ed.gov/admins/lead/account/compneedsassessment.pdf

Watkins, R., & Kaufman, R. (1996). An update of relating needs assessment and needs analysis. *Performance Improvement Journal, 35*(10), 10–13.

Witkin, B. R., & Altschuld, J.W. (1995). *Planning and conducting needs assessments: A practical guide.* Thousand Oaks, CA: Sage.

Additional Resources

Altschuld, J. W., & Kumar, D. D. (2010). *The needs assessment KIT—Book 1, needs assessment: An overview.* Thousand Oaks, CA: SAGE Publications.

Kaufman, R., & English, F. W. (1979). *Needs assessment: Concept and application.* Englewood Cliffs, NJ: Educational Technology Publications.

Kaufman, R., Rojas, A., & Mayer, H. (1993). *Needs assessment: A user's guide.* Englewood Cliffs, NJ: Educational Technology Publishers.

Watkins, R. & Kaufman, R. (2002). Assessing and evaluating: Differentiating perspectives. *Performance Improvement Journal, 41*(2), 22–28.

Watkins, R., West Meiers, M., & Visser, Y. (2012). *A guide to assessing needs: Tools for collecting information, making decisions, and achieving development results.* Washington, DC: World Bank.

seven
Symptoms and Underlying Causes

Symptoms, those you believe you recognize, seem to you irrational because you take them in an isolated manner, and you want to interpret them directly.

(Jacques Lacan, 1901–1981)

As discussed in Chapter 6, needs assessment identifies existing gaps in results and thus provides the basis for deriving useful and justifiable objectives, whereas needs analysis identifies what causes the needs and then identifies the solution requirements. Solution requirements are presupposed before fully specifying the actual problem to be solved and settling on a solution approach. This chapter focuses on the discussion of symptoms and underlying causes in the process of identifying the actual problem.

An Example

To bridge the digital divide, the government of a city launched a scheme to financially assist low-income families to purchase computers and home broadband connections. After three years, as a study showed, there had been a great improvement in school and home access to computers; however, the socioeconomic difference in students' computer usage at home persisted.

Consider the following questions:

- What led to this scheme?
- What problem did it solve?
- What new problem did it create?
- How was the new problem solved?

The solution first attempted to address the symptoms of the digital divide by providing financial assistance to low-income families for the purchase of computers and home broadband connections. School and home access to computers were improved, but the socioeconomic difference in students' computer usage at home remained unresolved. This effort pointed to an underlying cause involving the extent to which students were using computers and the quality of their use. Thus, it is important to look beyond symptoms to underlying causes since the symptoms are often only indications of a problem.

Symptoms, Problems and Causes

What is a symptom? In medical terminology, a symptom (from Greek συμπ τωμα, meaning *accident, misfortune, that which befalls*) is a departure from a normal function or feeling that is noticed by a patient, reflecting the presence of an unusual state or of a disease. A symptom is subjective, observed by the patient, and cannot be measured directly, whereas a medical sign is objective evidence of the presence of a disease or disorder as opposed to a symptom. Symptoms and signs are often non-specific, but often combinations of them are at least suggestive of specific diagnoses, helping to narrow down what may be wrong. For example, the Memorial Symptom Assessment Scale (MSAS) is a patient-rated instrument that was developed to provide multidimensional information about a diverse group of common symptoms (Portenoy et al., 1994). In general, a symptom is a phenomenon or circumstance accompanying some conditions, processes, feelings, etc., that can serve as evidence of something bad or undesirable, such as a problem or disease. In this chapter, a symptom of a problem is something that happens that can be considered as a sign or indication of a problem.

What people traditionally call problems are frequently only symptoms of problems. For example, the problem of *have or have-not* computer access is a symptom of the digital divide, which is the real problem. Defining a problem in terms of its symptoms obscures the real causes and can lead to symptomatic solutions that fail to correct the basic conditions causing the problem. However, addressing symptoms often produces short-term results, and, as a result, may be mistakenly considered a desirable approach. Problem symptoms and problem causes can look very much alike. Thus, it is important to distinguish between problem symptoms and problem causes, especially if one wishes to find long-term, sustainable solutions.

Problem symptoms are created by structural relationships among system components. Understanding these relationships helps discover the underlying causes of the problem, i.e. problem causes, and locate the points of leverage where patterns of behavior originate and can be changed. Problems are undesired results caused by structural relationships among system components. Thus, systems approach is most helpful in discovering the causes of problems. This is a complex process since the underlying causes of problems are seldom obvious and therefore specific problem solving technique is needed.

Test Your Understanding

To bridge the digital divide, the government of a city launched a scheme to financially assist low-income families to purchase computers and home broadband connections. This scheme was aimed at benefitting students from low-income families without any access, and the following services are provided to eligible families:

a. an economical Internet access service;
b. affordable computer equipment with flexible payment options;
c. technical support through a hotline and helpdesk;
d. training for students;
e. training for parents; and
f. group-based and one-on-one advisory services.

Which of these services are symptomatic solutions to the problem of digital inclusion or the problem of resolving the digital divide? Why?

Identifying the Problem and Underlying Causes

Root Cause Analysis (RCA), a popular method of problem solving, seeks to identify the origin of a problem using a specific set of steps, with associated tools, to find the underlying causes of the problem. RCA is a common tool for Total Quality Management (TQM). RCA assumes that systems and events are interrelated. An action in one area triggers an action in another, and another, and so on. By tracing back these actions, we can discover where the problem started and how it grew into the symptom we are facing. RCA looks at three types of causes—namely, (a) investigating the patterns of negative effects, (b) finding hidden flaws in the system, and (c) discovering specific actions that contributed to the problem. A simplified RCA process is described as follows (Jackson et al., n.d.—see Links):

Step One:
Describe the symptoms using all the specific facts and data available. Select the most significant problem symptom and ask: What do we see happening? What are the specific symptoms? Why is this occurring?

Step Two:
Identify any emerging patterns. Record and compile possible explanations, and ask: What proof do we have that the problem exists? What is the impact of the problem?

Step Three:
Continue the above two steps until the explanations converge into some fundamental causal factors. Focus on systemic explanations, and ask: What sequence of events leads to the problem? What conditions allow the problem to occur? What other problems surround the occurrence of the central problem?

Step Four:

Define the problem or problems by describing the root causes creating them. Identify the system structural relationships that are creating the conditions that need correcting, and ask: Why does the causal factor exist? What is the real reason the problem occurred?

Step Five:

Determine the action or actions needed to change the system relationships creating the problem or problems. Recommend and implement solutions, and ask: How will the solution be implemented? Who will be responsible for it? What are the risks of implementing the solution?

As an analytical tool, RCA is an essential way to perform a comprehensive, system-wide review of significant problems as well as the factors leading to those problems. The *seven basic tools of quality* (see https://en.wikipedia.org/wiki/Seven_Basic_Tools_of_Quality) is a set of graphical techniques identified as being most helpful in troubleshooting issues in the RCA process. It is a set of general tools useful for planning or controlling project quality in project management. These tools can be used to solve the vast majority of quality-related issues, and identify the underlying causes. The seven tools are: (1) Cause-and-effect diagram (also known as the fishbone diagram), (2) Check sheet, (3) Control chart, (4) Histogram, (5) Pareto chart, (6) Scatter diagram, and (7) Stratification (flow chart or run chart).

In sum, the gist of RCA is a multiple-questions process that provides a good reference to identify the causes underlying a problem. *Asking a question*, that is to say, placing a question mark at the end of a statement or raising the tone of voice to indicate asking rather than telling, can be easily done. However, *having a question*, which requires an admission of not knowing and then committing time and effort to a course of action to find out, is not an easy task. Evaluators and those conducting needs assessments and analyses are trained to have questions and persist in pursuing answers to the questions driving their assessments, analyses and evaluations.

A Problem Statement

Research involves systematic and sustained efforts aimed at understanding phenomena, predicting outcomes, explaining events, and/or furthering knowledge, whereas evaluation involves systematic and sustained efforts to support positive outcomes and determine the degree to which goals and desired outcomes have been met. Moreover, both evaluation and research processes involve asking good questions, admitting to not knowing, exploring alternative solution approaches and solutions, identifying the problem or the phenomenon to be evaluated or investigated, examining and analyzing evidence, and testing explanations and hypotheses—that is to say, both enterprises involve having questions, and both involve problem statements.

A problem statement is a factual description of the effects of a problem or a situation that leads to a perceived need. A problem statement serves as a guide to obtaining good answers—that is to say, effective solutions to identified problems. However, developing a good problem statement may be a difficult step in an evaluation or research process because at the beginning of an effort there may be inadequate or incomplete evidence and only vague or fuzzy descriptions of desired outcomes. However, adequate development of a problem statement is necessary to get the evaluation process underway. The extent of detail in problem identification may vary somewhat with the type of evaluation, and the nature of the problem and associated problem statement may change as an effort proceeds (see Chapter 10).

The development of an adequate problem statement for an evaluation effort involves reading, discussing, fact-finding, questioning and conceptualizing. Typically, the process is one of successive approximations to the problem as factors related to the problem are considered (Wiersma, 1995). The first step involves selecting an initial topic or area of interest. Then a specific statement of the problem is generated for that topic or interest area. In this part of the book and in this chapter, the basic terms 'symptom', 'problem' and 'cause' are used; it is important to understand and to be able to distinguish between symptoms, causes and problems. The following is an example that includes (1) an initial problem statement, (2) a restatement into a more manageable statement of the problem, and (3) questions to illustrate the identification of sub-problems.

Initial statement:

- The role of the technology coordinators in high schools should be clarified.

Restatement:

- A survey of the practices of the technology coordinators in the high schools of City H will serve to clarify that role.

Questions for sub-problems:

- What proportion of technology coordinators' working day is taken up with non-technology activities?
- What are the major strengths of technology coordinators' practices as perceived by teachers and students?
- What are the major weaknesses of technology coordinators' practices as perceived by teachers and students?
- What practices are perceived by technology coordinators as most effective in advising teachers and students about the use of technology?

In the above restatement of the problem, considerable effort to specify what is meant by or included in 'practice' would be necessary. The selected sub-problems also require definitions and further elaboration for specific situations. A good problem statement should provide the evaluator or researcher with a definite direction in pursuing the evaluation or research effort. The statement should indicate the general focus, the scope and the context of the problem. Finally, the problem statement should be concise and should identify the key factors (variables) of the evaluation/research study along with a framework for reporting results (see Chapter 10).

Learning Activities

A project seeks to evaluate the inequality in ICT use experienced by students with a view to identifying appropriate ways to address the problem of digital divide. A number of possible dimensions of factors were considered as follows: (1) background (e.g. gender, home conditions, ICT ownership); (2) access and use in and outside schools (e.g. types and frequency of use, social life, entertainment); (3) home-based use of ICT and its impact on educational attainment; (4) ICT use by teachers in teaching and learning (e.g. types and frequency of use in different subjects); (5) school ICT infrastructure and development; (6) school vision and policies on ICT development; (7) language proficiency among students and information access; (8) information literacy and digital skills of students to scrutinize quality of information access and use; (9) attitudes toward ICT-related ethical issues and societal impact; and (10) risk factors that can limit positive ICT impacts on education.

Given the scenario above, if you were the evaluator of this project, how would you proceed? How would you identify the problems and causes involved from the aforesaid possible factors?

Links

Symptom. (n.d.). In Wikipedia. Retrieved from https://en.wikipedia.org/wiki/Symptom

Jackson, K. et al. (n.d.). Root Cause Analysis: Tracing a Problem to its Origins. MindTools: Home/Problem Solving/Root Cause Analysis. Retrieved from www.mindtools.com/pages/article/newTMC_80.htm

Seven Basic Tools of Quality. (n.d.). In Wikipedia. Retrieved from https://en.wikipedia.org/wiki/Seven_Basic_Tools_of_Quality

Other Resources

Three sigma, Inc. Helping Executives Create and Sustain Superior Performance; see www.threesigma.com/

References

Portenoy, R. K., Thaler, H. T., Kornblith, A. B., Lepore, J. M., Friedlander-Klar, H., Kiyasu, E., Sobel, K., Coyle, N., Kemeny, N., Norton, L. & Scher, H. (1994). The Memorial Symptom Assessment Scale: An instrument for the evaluation of symptom prevalence, characteristics and distress. *European Journal of Cancer*, 30(9), 1326–1336.

Wiersma, W. (1995). *Research methods in education* (6th ed.). Boston, MA: Allyn & Bacon.

Additional Resources

Fitzpatrick, J. L., Sanders, J. R., & Worthen, B. R. (2011). *Program evaluation: Alternative approaches and practical guidelines* (4th ed.). Upper Saddle River, NJ: Pearson Education.

Hamilton, J., & Feldman, J. (2014). Planning a program evaluation: Matching methodology to program status. In J. M. Spector, M. D. Merrill, J. Elen, & M. J. Bishop (Eds.), *Handbook of research on educational communications and technology* (4th ed., pp. 249–256). New York: Springer.

Kaufman, R. (1988). Preparing useful performance indicators. *Training and Development Journal, 42*(9), 80–83.

Kaufman, R., Keller, J., & Watkins, R. (1996). What works and what doesn't: Evaluation beyond Kirkpatrick. *Performance+ Instruction, 35*(2), 8–12.

Mertens, D. M., & Wilson, A. T. (2012). *Program evaluation theory and practice: A comprehensive guide.* New York: Guilford Press.

Oppenheim, A. N. (1992). *Questionnaire design and attitude measurement.* London: Pinter Publishers.

Owston, R. (2007). Contextual factors that sustain innovative pedagogical practice using technology: An international study. *Journal of Educational Change, 8*(1), 61–77.

Owston, R. (2008). Models and methods for evaluation. In J. M. Spector, M. D. Merrill, J. J G. van Merriënboer, & M. P. Driscoll (Eds.) *Handbook of research on educational communications and technology* (3rd ed.; pp. 605–617). New York: Routledge.

Petrosino, A. (2000). Answering the why question in evaluation: The causal-model approach. *Canadian Journal of Program Evaluation, 15*(1), 1–24.

Rogers, P. J., Petrosino, A., Huebner, T. A., & Hacsi, T. A. (2000). Program theory evaluation: Practice, promise, and problems. *New directions for evaluation, 2000*(87), 5–13.

Rooney, J. J., & Heuvel, L. N. V. (2004). Root cause analysis for beginners. Quality Progress, July 2004, pp. 45–53. Retrieved from https://servicelink.pinnacol.com/pinnacol_docs/lp/cdrom_web/safety/management/accident_investigation/Root_Cause.pdf

Spector, J. M. (2014). Program and project evaluation. In J. M. Spector, M. D. Merrill, J. Elen, & M. J. Bishop (Eds.). *Handbook of research on educational communications and technology* (4th ed.; pp. 195–201). New York: Springer.

Zikmund, W. (1997). *Business research methods* (5th ed.). Orlando, FL: Harcourt College.

eight
A Theory of Change

Change is the law of life. And those who look only to the past or present are certain to miss the future.

(John F. Kennedy, 1917–1963)

In Chapter 7, the symptoms and underlying causes of problems to be addressed in a program/project evaluation were discussed. Moreover, a set of beliefs about how a program/project works or why a problem occurs is crucial. Assumptions about resources and activities and how these are expected to lead to intended outcomes are often referred to as program theory, and a logic model is a useful tool for describing program theory (McLaughlin & Jordan, 2010).

Background

Carol Weiss was one of the first theorists to bring attention to the need for testing the underlying assumptions about why a program should work in evaluation. In her seminal work on evaluation practice entitled *Evaluation research: Methods of assessing program effectiveness* (1972), Weiss talks about creating a model of the program's causal processes and testing it in the evaluation. She also describes two types of variables that should be examined in evaluation, namely, program operation variables and bridging variables. Program operation variables are those that describe how the intervention operates, such as frequency, duration, and quality of contact, whereas bridging variables are those that link the program operation variables to desired outcomes. Weiss uses what she calls a *process model* to describe how these variables can be integrated and serve as candidates for testing in the evaluation (Petrosino, 2000).

Theory-based Evaluation

Theory-based evaluation has developed significantly since Weiss's article was published in 1997. She pointed to theory-based evaluation being mostly used in the areas of health promotion and risk prevention. Now, the use of program theory is commonplace, and her work has been cited in a wide range of evaluation (Rogers, 2007). Weiss (1997) places emphasis on linking specific program activities to specific mechanisms, and she argues that measurements should track and monitor the steps of the program as it develops and is implemented. Similar to her discrimination between program operation and bridging variables, Weiss (1972) further distinguishes between implementation theory and program theory. Implementation theory involves the activities or tasks the program is going to accomplish, whereas program theory encompasses the mechanisms for change that the activities or tasks will bring about or are intended to bring about. Moreover, both implementation theory and program theory comprise the program's overall *theory of change* (Petrosino, 2000).

Along with this development of theory-based evaluation has come a proliferation of terminology. However, Weiss used the terms 'program theory' and 'logic model' to refer to essentially similar concepts. Now there is a much longer list of labels that have been used, not with consistently distinct definitions, including theory-based, theory-driven, theory-oriented, theory-anchored, theory-of-change, intervention theory, outcomes hierarchies, program theory and program logic (Rogers, 2007).

Theory-driven Evaluation

Theory-driven evaluation is a contextual or holistic assessment of a program based on the conceptual framework of program theory. The purpose of theory-driven evaluation is to provide information on not only the performance or merit of a program but on how and why the program achieves such a result. Program theory is a set of implicit or explicit assumptions of how the program should be organized and why the program is expected to work (Chen, 2005). The types of program theory are introduced in the following section. When looking into the crucial assumptions underlying a program, evaluators should consider that theory-driven evaluation provides insightful information that assists stakeholders in understanding those components of the program that work well and those that do not. Theory-driven evaluation is particularly useful when stakeholders want an evaluation to serve both accountability (summative) and program improvement (formative) needs (Chen, 2005).

Petrosino (2000) suggests using the term 'causal-model evaluation' rather than 'theory-driven evaluation', and argues that emphasizing causes accurately describes what most evaluators and theorists mean, namely that the evaluation is testing the causes that explain how the program intends to achieve its outcomes. The idea of basing program evaluation on a causal model is not a new one. Most program theories are summarized in a causal chain (Rogers, Petrosino, Huebner, & Hacsi, 2000). A theory is a plausible or scientifically acceptable general principle or body of principles offered to explain phenomena or a hypothesis assumed for the sake of investigation and testing. Similarly, a program theory is a set of implicit or explicit assumptions that represents a plausible explanation of how the program should be organized and why the program can be expected to work (Chen, 2005).

Theory-based and theory-driven evaluation both appear to be appropriate and acceptable descriptive terms for an evaluation. The differences are minor from the perspective of practitioners. Theory-based evaluation is perhaps more acceptable in practitioner communities whereas theory-driven evaluation is possibly preferred by academic and research communities, although both terms have users in the various evaluation communities.

Test Your Understanding

Which of the following are the focuses of theory-based evaluation of a program?

a. program dissemination;
b. specific program activities to specific mechanisms;
c. measurement should track the steps of the program; or
d. program delivery system.

Which of the following is not related directly to the purposes of theory-driven evaluation of a program?

a. performance of a program;
b. merit of a program;
c. whether the program is innovative;
d. how the program achieves such a result; or
e. why the program achieves such a result.

Program Theory and Promises

Program theory has been seen as an answer to many different problems in evaluation. Here we briefly discuss the types of program theory and areas where program theory has been seen as promising. We caution developers against promising more than can be delivered or reasonably evaluated. Possibilities are not co-extensive with promises, and planners, implementers, policymakers and evaluators should be focused on realistic promises. Program theory and a theory of change can assist in making promises clear, explicit and reasonable.

Types of Program Theory

Program theory may be developed by a principal investigator or project director, but it is often developed by an evaluator based on (a) a review of the research literature pertaining to similar programs and relevant causal mechanisms, (b) discussions with key informants, (c) a review of program documentation, or (d) observations of the program as it is planned and evolves. Program theory may also be developed by the stakeholders of the program, often through a group process. Many practitioners advise using a combination of these approaches so as to avoid a mismatch between the expectations of stakeholders and those of the personnel involved in planning and implementing the effort. Program theory can be developed before an effort is implemented or after it is underway; moreover, program theory may be modified as an effort unfolds. Program theory can be used to change plans and practice as the effort develops.

While there are many variations of program theory, Rogers and colleagues (2000) identify three main types in terms of their complexity and detail. A simple program theory shows a single intermediate outcome by which the program achieves its ultimate outcome. More complex program theories show a series of intermediate outcomes, sometimes in multiple strands that combine to cause the ultimate outcomes. The third type of program theory is represented by a series of boxes labeled inputs, processes, outputs, and outcomes, with arrows connecting them. The different components of this type of program theory are simply listed in each box though it does not show the relationships among different components or specify which processes lead to which outputs. However, these relationships are sometimes explored in the empirical component of the evaluation (Rogers et al., 2000) and can be visually represented in the form of a *logic model* (see Chapter 12).

Promises and Benefits

The most fascinating promise made for program theory in evaluation is that it provides relevant clues to answer the question of why programs work or fail to work. Consider the usual practice of trying to understand why programs do or do not work. Following the analysis and reporting of results, evaluators usually work in a post hoc manner to suggest reasons for the observed results (Petrosino, 2000).

Program theory has been used by evaluators to develop better evidence for attributing outcomes to a program in the context of implementation. Thus, another promise made for program theory is better evidence for causal attribution to answer the question of whether the program caused the observed outcomes (Rogers et al., 2000).

Many of the claims for the benefits of program theory refer to its capacity to improve programs directly or indirectly. Articulating a program theory can expose flawed thinking about why the effort should work and, as a result, guide corrections early in an effort, which is far more efficient than returning design and development after a full-scale implementation. The process of developing a program theory can itself be a rewarding experience, as project staff develop common understanding of their work and identify the most important components (Rogers et al., 2000).

Test Your Understanding

Which of the following is not a benefit of program theory in evaluation?

   a. to offer capacity to improve programs;
   b. to provide some clues to answer the question of why programs work;
   c. to identify possible solutions; or
   d. to give evidence for causal attribution.

Theories of Change and Logic Models

There are different modes and manifestations of theory-based or theory-driven evaluation. In this chapter, the focus is on the relationship of a theory of change and a logic model (see Chapter 12 for a more detailed discussion of logic models).

A logical framework or logic model is a tool for planning and managing development projects; it looks like a table and structures components of a project in a clear, concise, organized and logical way. A logic model displays the sequence of actions in a program, depicts what the program is and will do, and illustrates how investments or activities will be linked to results or outcomes (Mertens & Wilson, 2012).

A logic model portrays a current situation and the associated problem, the implementation of an intervention intended to address the problem situation, and the projected or predicted outcomes and benefits of that intervention if successfully implemented. A theory of change that would explain why and how the intervention would lead from the problem state to the desired outcomes is normally associated with and depicted in a logic model (Spector, 2014). One key value of a logic model is that it displays the chain of connections showing how a program is expected to work to achieve desired results. Part III of this book provides additional details about logic models and implementations.

A logic model conveys the story of the effort to be evaluated by showing links between inputs, activities and outcomes. In short, a logic model depicts a theory of change or program theory. Figure 8.1 presents an evaluation framework with a focus on a theory of change. The various components in this framework, some of which have been discussed in previous chapters with others to be discussed in subsequent chapters, include:

   • types of educational technology efforts to be evaluated (e.g., project, program, product, practice, policy);
   • methods and instruments involved (e.g., surveys, interviews, direct observations, document reviews);
   • data to be analyzed (e.g., quantitative, qualitative, both);
   • focus and scope of the evaluation (e.g., foundation domain, design domain, production domain, implementation domain, maintenance domain);
   • type of evaluation being conducted (e.g., formative, summative, confirmatory);

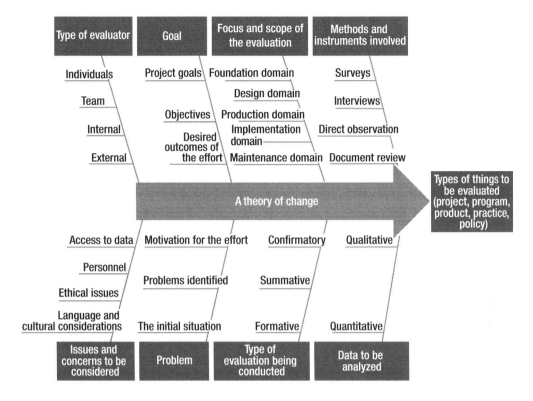

FIGURE 8.1 An Evaluation Framework

- goal (e.g., goals, objectives, desired outcomes of the effort);
- problem (e.g., the initial situation, problems identified, motivation for the effort);
- type of evaluator (e.g., individual, team, internal, external); and
- issues and concerns to be considered (e.g., access to data, personnel, ethical issues, language and cultural considerations).

Figure 8.1 is an alternative representation of Figure 3.1 that depicted a general framework for educational technology evaluation.

Learning Activities

A cluster of 12 special schools in a city, serving students with different kinds of special needs, has decided to initiate a project in order to (a) develop an e-learning platform to meet the needs of a diverse population of students, (b) give teachers flexible access to information and pedagogical resources, and (c) help principals better manage their schools.

If you were asked to develop a theory of change to explain why and how the effort would lead from the problem state to the desired outcomes, what else would you need to know? How would you gather that information? Finally, what would be the essential components you would consider in a theory of change that would or could explain how the effort can be expected to attain its goals and, afterwards, to what extent the effort succeeded?

Links

Theory. (n.d.). In Wikipedia. Retrieved from https://en.wikipedia.org/wiki/Theory

Theory. (n.d.). In Merriam-Webster Dictionary. Retrieved from www.merriam-webster.com/dictionary/theory

References

Chen, H. T. (2005). Theory-driven evaluation. In S. Mathison (Ed.), *Encyclopedia of evaluation* (pp. 415–419). Thousand Oaks, CA: Sage.

McLaughlin, J.A., & Jordan, G.B. (2010), Using logic models. In J. S. Wholey, H. P. Hatry, & K. E. Newcomer (Eds.) *Handbook of Practical Program Evaluation* (3rd ed.). Hoboken, NJ: John Wiley & Sons.

Mertens, D. M., & Wilson, A. T. (2012). *Program evaluation theory and practice: A comprehensive guide.* New York: Guilford Press.

Petrosino, A. (2000). Answering the why question in evaluation: The causal-model approach. *Canadian Journal of Program Evaluation*, 15(1), 1–24.

Rogers, P. J. (2007). Theory-based evaluation: Reflections ten years on. In Mathison, S. (Ed.). *Enduring issues in evaluation: The 20th anniversary of the collaboration between NDE and AEA*. New directions for evaluation. Vol. 114 (pp. 63–67). San Francisco, CA: Jossey-Bass Publishers and the American Evaluation Association.

Rogers, P. J., Petrosino, A., Huebner, T. A., & Hacsi, T. A. (2000). Program theory evaluation: Practice, promise, and problems. *New Directions for Evaluation*, 2000(87), 5–13.

Spector, J. M. (2014). Program and project evaluation. In J. M. Spector, M. D. Merrill, J. Elen, & M. J. Bishop (Eds.). *Handbook of research on educational communications and technology* (4th ed.; pp. 195–201). New York: Springer.

Weiss, C. H. (1972). *Evaluation research: Methods for assessing program effectiveness.* Englewood Cliffs, NJ: Prentice-Hall.

Weiss, C.H. (1997). Theory-based evaluation: Past, present, and future. *New Directions for Evaluation*, 76, 41–55.

Additional Resources

Fitzpatrick, J. L., Sanders, J. R., & Worthen, B. R. (2011). *Program evaluation: Alternative approaches and practical guidelines* (4th ed.). Upper Saddle River, NJ: Pearson Education.

Hamilton, J., & Feldman, J. (2014). Planning a program evaluation: Matching methodology to program status. In J. M. Spector, M. D. Merrill, Jan Elen, & M. J. Bishop (Eds.), *Handbook of research on educational communications and technology* (4th ed., pp. 249–256). New York: Springer.

Kaufman, R. (1988). Preparing useful performance indicators. *Training and Development Journal*, 42(9), 80–83.

Kaufman, R., Keller, J., & Watkins, R. (1996). What works and what doesn't: Evaluation beyond Kirkpatrick. *Performance+ Instruction*, 35(2), 8–12.

Oppenheim, A. N. (1992). *Questionnaire design and attitude measurement.* London: Pinter Publishers.

Owston, R. (2007). Contextual factors that sustain innovative pedagogical practice using technology: An international study. *Journal of Educational Change*, 8(1), 61–77.

Owston, R. (2008). Models and methods for evaluation. In J. M. Spector, M. D. Merrill, J. J. G. van Merriënboer, & M. P. Driscoll (Eds.) *Handbook of research on educational communications and technology* (3rd ed.; pp. 605–617). New York: Routledge.

Portenoy, R. K., Thaler, H. T., Kornblith, A. B., Lepore, J. M., Friedlander-Klar, H., Kiyasu, E., Sobel, K., Coyle, N., Kemeny, N., Norton, L., & Scher, H. (1994). The memorial symptom assessment scale: An instrument for the evaluation of symptom prevalence, characteristics and distress. *European Journal of Cancer, 30A*(9), 1326–1336.

Rooney, J. J., & Heuvel, L. N. V. (2004). Root cause analysis for beginners. *Quality Progress*, July 2004, pp. 45–53. Retrieved from https://servicelink.pinnacol.com/pinnacol_docs/lp/cdrom_web/safety/management/accident_investigation/Root_Cause.pdf

Wiersma, W. (1995). *Research methods in education* (6th ed.). Boston, MA: Allyn & Bacon.

Zikmund, W. (1997). *Business research methods* (5th ed.). Orlando, FL: Harcourt College.

nine
Outcome Measures and Indicators

There are two possible outcomes: if the result confirms the hypothesis, then you've made a measurement. If the result is contrary to the hypothesis, then you've made a discovery.
(Enrico Fermi, 1901–1954)

It is possible to measure an object, such as a table, with either edge of a dual-scale ruler. One edge of a dual-scale rule has inches and the other has centimeters, so that the units of measurement will vary, depending on which edge is used. Many measurement problems in evaluation and research are similar to the dual-scale ruler in the sense that there are often alternative scales of measurement. The researcher or evaluator has the opportunity to select a measuring system. However, unlike the two-edged ruler, many measurement scales in evaluation or research are not often directly comparable (Zikmund, 1997). The first question the evaluator/researcher must ask: What is to be measured?

What is a Measure?

Suppose that we wish to know the length of a table. We may then take a metal ruler, hold it against the longer edge of the table, and read off the answer (say 35 inches). This measure has, in principle, two components: the *true* measure and a second component, which we may call *error* (Oppenheim, 1992). We shall, for the moment, ignore the kinds of errors-of-observation and notation that may arise because we have been a little careless or imprecise, and draw attention to the fact that we have used a metal ruler. Since we know that metal expands or contracts under different temperature conditions, part of our answer is not a measure of length but a measure of temperature. Since, at this point,

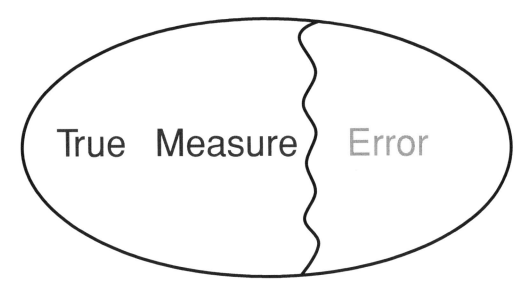

FIGURE 9.1 Measure and Error

we are not interested in temperature, we regard this aspect of the measure as error in the sense that it is irrelevant to what we need. Thus, any measure could be represented as shown in two components: measure and error, as depicted in Figure 9.1.

Figure 9.1 is an abstract representation. It suggests that we know a measure is impure or inexact but not always by how much or in what way (Oppenheim, 1992). A measure may be contaminated by aspects or events even that are not relevant to the effort. For example, an after school program might be devised to improve the graduation rate. As the effort is being developed, a sudden and unexpected influx of non-native speaking immigrants are registered in the school and require more than the average time to graduate. A simple graduation rate measure may suggest that the effort result in a lowered graduation rate. A more sophisticated graduation rate measure that accounted for the recent non-native speaking students might suggest otherwise. If one accepts the WYMIWYG ('whim-ee-whig'; what you measure is what you get) principle, then what is measured and how it is measured are very important.

Types of Data and Measurement Scales

Given a large number of variables in an evaluation or research study, measurement error creates difficulties in identifying significant associations among variables (Weiss, 1997). Precise measurement in evaluation or research requires a careful conceptual definition, an operational definition, and a system of consistent rules for assigning scores or numbers. A concept is a generalized idea about a class of objects, attributes, occurrences, or processes, and an operational definition gives meaning to a concept by specifying the activities or operations necessary in order to measure it.

In the social sciences, scaling is the process of measuring or ordering entities with respect to quantitative attributes. In other words, a scale represents a spectrum or series of categories, and the purpose of scaling is to represent an item's, a person's or an event's place in the spectrum or series. In evaluation and research there are many different scales. It is traditional to classify scales of measurement on the basis of the mathematical comparisons that are allowable with these scales. The four types of scales are nominal, ordinal, interval and ratio (Zikmund, 1997).

A nominal scale is the simplest type of scale. The numbers or letters assigned to objects serve as labels for identification or classification. An example of a typical nominal scale in evaluation/research is the coding of males as 1 and females as 2. An ordinal scale arranges objects or alternatives according to their magnitude in an ordered relationship. When respondents are asked to rank order their preferences, ordinal values are assigned. A typical ordinal scale in evaluation/research asks respondents to rate their perceived proficiency in using a computer or other educational technology as "excellent," "good," "fair," or "poor." We know "excellent" is higher than "good," but we do not know by how much.

Interval scales not only indicate order, they also measure order (or distance) in units of equal intervals. Moreover, the location of the zero point is arbitrary. For example, in the calculation of consumer price index, if the base year is 1997, the price level during 1997 will be set at 100. Although this is an equal-interval measurement scale, the zero point is arbitrary. Another example of an interval scale is the Fahrenheit temperature scale. Due to the lack of an absolute zero point, the Fahrenheit interval scale does not allow the conclusion that 40°F is four times as warm or great as 10°F, only that the interval distance is four times greater. Similarly, when an interval scale is used to measure psychological attributes, the researcher can comment on the magnitude of differences or compare the average differences on attributes that are measured but cannot determine the actual strength of attitudes toward an object. However, changes in concepts over time can be compared if the researcher continues to use the same scale in longitudinal research. Ratio scales have absolute rather than relative quantities. For example, money and weight are ratio scales because they possess an absolute zero and interval properties. The absolute zero represents a point on the scale where there is an absence of the given attribute. However, for most behavioral research, interval scales are typically used in measurement. A summary of numerical operations and descriptive statistics for types of scales is presented in Table 9.1 (see Zikmund, 1997).

Test Your Understanding

Which of the following is an example of an interval scale and why?

a. preference ranking
b. time of day on a 12-hour clock
c. weight of students
d. internet user types

Table 9.1 Numerical scales and associated statistics

Type of scale	Numerical Operation	Descriptive Statistics
Nominal	Counting	Frequency in each category
		Percentage in each category
		Mode
Ordinal	Ranking ordering	Median
		Range
		Percentile ranking
Interval	Arithmetic operations on intervals between numbers	Mean
		Standard deviation
		Variance
Ratio	Arithmetic operations on actual quantities	Geometric mean
		Coefficient of variation

Note: All statistics that are appropriate for lower-order scales (nominal is the lowest) are appropriate for higher-order scales (ratio is the highest).

Criteria for Quality in Data Collection

The quality of data collection is of paramount importance for evaluators to reach accurate conclusions about the functioning and effectiveness of a program/project. Reliability and **validity** are the most common terms related to quantitative data collection. Evaluators have developed parallel criteria for the quality of qualitative evaluations: dependability instead of reliability, and credibility instead of validity (Lincoln & Guba, 2000).

Reliability and Dependability

Reliability means consistency, and adequate reliability is a precondition to validity. Reliability or consistency is never perfect; it is always a matter of degree. Reliability may be measured in several different ways. For quantitative data collection, an evaluator repeatedly administers the instrument to the same sample within a short period. This is called test–retest reliability. However, this may produce resistance, as well as a practice effect; in a sense, it will no longer be the same test being administered under the same conditions in intensive test–retest procedures. To avoid these problems one can use the internal consistency method, usually associated with statistics such as Cronbach's alpha or the Kuder-Richardson formula. For quantitative observational data, two observers' data are compared to see whether they are consistently recording the same behaviors when they view the same events. This is called inter-rater reliability. Intra-rater reliability is used to determine whether a single observer is consistently recording data over a period of time (Mertens & Wilson, 2012; Oppenheim, 1992).

In qualitative studies, changes are to be expected. The evaluator needs to develop a system for documenting what changes occur at what points during the study and for what reasons. This can be done by keeping a protocol log that enables the conduct of a dependability audit that involves reviewing project records to determine the extent to which project procedures and changes are documented (Mertens & Wilson, 2012).

Validity and credibility

Validity refers to how well a test or measure in fact reflects what it is supposed to measure. The higher the validity, the more credible the measure, and the more confidence one can place in a finding associated with the measure. There are different forms of evidence to support validity in quantitative data collection. Construct validity shows how well the test links up with a set of theoretical assumptions about an abstract construct such as intelligence. Content validity seeks to establish that the items or questions are a well-balanced sample of the content domain to be measured. Predictive validity shows how well the test can forecast some future event or situation such as job performance or future examination attainment. Concurrent validity shows how well the test correlates with other, well-validated measures of the same topic, administered at about the same time (Oppenheim, 1992; Mertens & Wilson, 2012).

In qualitative data collection, the credibility question is framed as whether there is a correspondence between the way respondents actually perceive the social constructs and the way the evaluator portrays the respondents' viewpoints. Strategies to enhance credibility include (a) prolonged and substantial engagement, (b) persistent observations, (c) peer debriefing, (d) progressive subjectivity, (e) member checking, and (f) multiple data sources (Mertens & Wilson, 2012).

Test Your Understanding

Consider the following example about the difference between reliability and validity of a common bathroom scale.

If someone who is 150 pounds steps on a scale (weight measuring device in this example) five times and gets readings of "15," "120," "95," "140," and "200," then:

   a. the scale is not reliable;
   b. the scale is not valid;
   c. the scale is reliable, but not valid;
   d. the scale is not reliable, but valid;
   e. the scale is both reliable and valid; or
   f. the scale is neither reliable nor valid.

If someone who is 150 pounds steps on a scale five times and the scale consistently reads "120," then:

   a. the scale is not reliable;
   b. the scale is not valid;
   c. the scale is reliable, but not valid;

d. the scale is not reliable, but valid;

e. the scale is both reliable and valid; or

f. the scale is neither reliable nor valid.

If someone who is 150 pounds steps on a scale 5 times and the scale reads "150" each time, then:

a. the scale is not reliable;

b. The scale is not valid;

c. the scale is reliable, but not valid;

d. the scale is not reliable, but valid;

e. the scale is both reliable and valid; or

f. the scale is neither reliable nor valid.

Indicators

"An indicator is a pointer. It can be a measurement, a number, a fact, an opinion or a perception that directs attention to a specific condition or situation. It measures changes in that condition or situation over time" (UNIFEM, 2009, p. 29). How do stakeholders know whether the evidence presented to them from data collection indicates the extent to which a program succeeded or failed? To answer this question, indicators provide a close look at the results of initiatives and actions. Moreover, the difference between an indicator and a statistic is that using indicators typically involves comparison with a norm or standard. Thus, evaluators encourage stakeholders to give thought to the performance indicators that they would accept as evidence of the program's success or failure (Mertens & Wilson, 2012).

Performance indicators are sometimes also called performance targets or benchmarks. They specify the level of outcome attainment stakeholders expected or hoped for, for example how many grade-level increases in reading ability. It is often best to set performance targets based on past performance. Therefore, you may want to wait until you have some baseline outcome data before determining performance targets. However, if you do not have extra time to collect baseline data, you can set initial performance targets based on levels attained in comparable or related programs (Mertens & Wilson, 2012).

Defining a good performance indicator requires careful analysis of what is to be measured, and a distinction between outputs and outcomes. An output measure is a calculation, recording or tabulation of the results of an activity, effort or process that can be expressed in numerical or non-numerical data. Outcomes measurement is a way of measuring the treatment provided to a subject and the subject's responses to each treatment. Outcome indicators measure how well initiatives are accomplishing their intended results; they compare the result of an intervention to the situation beforehand, whereas process indicators measure how well activities are being conducted. Process measures track how much is being done and how well people like what is being done. Example process (output) measures include the number of people who attended a training session and participant satisfaction ratings of the training session. Both outcome and process indicators are tools stakeholders can use to gauge the success of the effort being evaluated.

Learning Activities

The following are simplified examples of performance indicators for the two types of results (outputs and outcomes):

a. Upon completion of vocational educational training, at least 80 percent of all those finishing the program will get a job in one of their first three occupational choices, keep that job for at least one year and have an income that at least equals or exceeds the median salary.

b. At least 85 percent of all full-time students in the "Individualized High School Learning Program" will meet all completion requirements and graduate after no more than four years of full-time enrollment.

Which one is an output performance indicator? Which one is an outcome performance indicator?

Links

Measurement. (n.d.). In Wikipedia. Retrieved from www.en.wikipedia.org/wiki/Measurement

Observational error. (n.d.). In Wikipedia. Retrieved from www.en.wikipedia.org/wiki/Observational_error

Performance indicator. (n.d.). In Wikipedia. Retrieved from www.en.wikipedia.org/wiki/Performance_indicator

Other Resources

Three sigma, Inc. Helping Executives Create and Sustain Superior Performance; see www.threesigma.com/

References

Lincoln, Y. S. & Guba, E. G. (2000). Paradigmatic controversies, contradictions and emerging confluences. In N.K. Denzin & Y.S. Lincoln (Eds.), Handbook of Qualitative Research (2nd ed., pp. 163–188). Thousand Oaks, CA: Sage.

Mertens, D. M., & Wilson, A. T. (2012). *Program evaluation theory and practice: A comprehensive guide.* New York: Guilford Press.

Oppenheim, A. N. (1992). *Questionnaire design and attitude measurement.* London: Pinter Publishers.

United Nations Development Fund for Women (UNIFEM). (2009, July). *EU gender politics in an international context—Gender perspectives and gender indicators.* Report from the international WOMNET conference, Berlin, Germany.

Weiss, C. H. (1997). Theory-based evaluation: Past, present, and future. *New Directions for Evaluation, 76,* 41–55.

Zikmund, W. (1997). *Business research methods* (5th ed.). Orlando, FL: Harcourt College.

Additional Resources

Fitzpatrick, J. L., Sanders, J. R., & Worthen, B. R. (2011). *Program evaluation: alternative approaches and practical guidelines* (4th ed.). Upper Saddle River, NJ: Pearson Education.

Hamilton, J., & Feldman, J. (2014). Planning a program evaluation: Matching methodology to program status. In J. M. Spector, M. D. Merrill, J. Elen, & M. J. Bishop (Eds.), *Handbook of research on educational communications and technology* (4th ed.; pp. 249–256). New York: Springer.

Kaufman, R. (1988). Preparing Useful Performance Indicators. *Training and Development Journal, 42*(9), 80–83.

Kaufman, R., Keller, J., & Watkins, R. (1996). What works and what doesn't: Evaluation beyond Kirkpatrick. *Performance+ Instruction, 35*(2), 8–12.

Owston, R. (2007). Contextual factors that sustain innovative pedagogical practice using technology: An international study. *Journal of Educational Change, 8*(1), 61–77.

Owston, R. (2008). Models and methods for evaluation. In J. M. Spector, M. D. Merrill, J. J G. van Merriënboer, & M. P. Driscoll (Eds.) *Handbook of research on educational communications and technology* (3rd ed.; pp. 605–617). New York: Routledge.

Petrosino, A. (2000). Answering the why question in evaluation: The causal-model approach. *Canadian Journal of Program Evaluation, 15*(1), 1–24.

Portenoy, R. K., Thaler, H. T., Kornblith, A. B., Lepore, J. M., Friedlander-Klar, H., Kiyasu, E., Sobel, K., Coyle, N., Kemeny, N., Norton, L., & Scher, H. (1994). The memorial symptom assessment scale: An instrument for the evaluation of symptom prevalence, characteristics and distress. *European Journal of Cancer, 30*(9), 1326–1336.

Rogers, P. J., Petrosino, A., Huebner, T. A., & Hacsi, T. A. (2000). Program theory evaluation: Practice, promise, and problems. *New directions for evaluation, 2000*(87), 5–13.

Rooney, J. J., & Heuvel, L. N. V. (2004). Root cause analysis for beginners. *Quality Progress,* July 2004, 45–53.

Spector, J. M. (2014). Program and project evaluation. In J. M. Spector, M. D. Merrill, J. Elen, & M. J. Bishop (Eds.). *Handbook of research on educational communications and technology* (4th ed.; pp. 195–201). New York: Springer.

Wiersma, W. (1995). *Research methods in education* (6th ed.). Boston, MA: Allyn & Bacon.

ten
Mediators, Moderators and Contextual Factors

To be is to be the value of a variable.
(Willard Van Orman Quine, 1908–2000)

Variables are constructs that take on different values, and are what is measured or manipulated in research and evaluation. This chapter discusses moderators and mediators, which are important variables in research and evaluation, along with contextual variables, as these are all important variables to consider when analyzing and interpreting findings.

Evaluation Purpose and Design

Owston (2008), in the context of program evaluation, presented six common evaluation purposes including (1) attainment of the effort's goals and objectives, (2) improvement, (3) accreditation, (4) development of theory about intervention, (5) meeting information needs of diverse audiences, and (6) overall impact. As previously discussed, the evaluator needs to identify the stakeholders and find out what their expectations are for the evaluation and the kind of information they seek about the effort. The evaluator then decides upon the actual design of the evaluation study.

A design of study is simply a plan for conducting research or an evaluation. It is a blueprint for how the research or evaluation will be conducted. Fitzpatrick, Sanders and Worthen (2011) summarize three types of commonly used designs: (a) descriptive designs (case study, cross-sectional, time-series), (b) causal designs (pre-post, posttest-only), and (c) quasi-experimental designs (interrupted time-series, comparison group, case study).

In connection with these designs, their characteristics, purposes and sample questions to be addressed are also to be considered. Selecting the appropriate design and working through and completing a well thought out logic plan provides a strong foundation for achieving a successful evaluation. Evaluators may use many designs and methods in their evaluation studies. The choice should be based on the methods that are most appropriate for answering the questions being asked, the context of the efforts including the current state of affairs and the desired outcomes, and the values and information needs of the stakeholders.

Descriptive designs are the most common designs in evaluation and serve many useful purposes. Cross-sectional designs provide useful quantitative information on large numbers of individuals and groups. Case studies are valuable for exploring issues in depth, providing thick descriptions of programs in implementation, different outcomes, contextual issues, and needs and perspectives of various stakeholders. Time-series designs are effective in describing changes over time. If the purposes of an evaluation question are causal, evaluators should carefully discuss expectations and implications with stakeholders. Design choices also include experimental, quasi-experimental, and explanatory case study designs (Fitzpatrick et al., 2011). Moreover, designs often are mixed to serve the purposes of the evaluation and needs of stakeholders (see Chapter 6).

Design and Data Collection

Once the basic design of the evaluation study is established, the next decision is to determine data sources and methods to gather the data. To answer most evaluation questions, data will be gathered from the entire population if the population of interest is relatively small or from a representative sample if the population is large. Methods of random sampling can be used when the group is large and generalizability is important. Purposive sampling is useful when the evaluation can benefit from information from a particular, identified subgroup to learn more about that group. Purposive sampling is often used in conducting intensive interviews and in case studies.

Design of study and data collection method are two distinct and separate concepts. No specific design must be accompanied by a specific data collection method. There are choices and decisions to be made. A number of constraints (time, funds, etc.) and other local considerations (e.g., availability of people) can influence a choice with regard to the method of collecting data. A data collection method is selected after a design has been established.

Data collection is the process of gathering and measuring information on variables of interest in an established and systematic fashion that enables one to answer evaluation questions. The goal for data collection is to capture quality evidence that then translates to rich data analysis and allows the building of a convincing and credible answer to questions that have been posed. A formal data collection process is necessary as it ensures that data gathered are both defined and accurate and that subsequent decisions based on arguments embodied in the findings are valid. Fitzpatrick and colleagues

(2011) provide a summary of data collection methods, including documents, records, observation, surveys, telephone interviews, electronic interviews or surveys, focus groups, and tests. Each data collection method has its important characteristics and might be used to address particular evaluation questions.

In the collected data, a constant is a characteristic or condition that is the same for all individuals in a study. A variable is a characteristic that takes on different values or conditions for different individuals. Independent and dependent variables are descriptors of variables commonly used in educational evaluation. The independent variables may be affecting the dependent variables, and in that sense, dependent variables depend on independent variables. In an evaluation, the intervention is the main independent variable that is being manipulated. The intervention is something that only participants in the treatment group are given. Participants in the control or comparison groups do not receive the intervention.

Test Your Understanding

If the purpose is to determine the primary reasons that students miss school, which of the following data sources and methods is not appropriate?

a. school records of absences;
b. teacher interviews;
c. interviews with students with excessive absences and their parents;
d. interviews with mathematics teachers; or
e. survey of students.

Which of the following descriptions is not correct?

a. In an experiment, the independent variable is the variable being manipulated or changed.
b. In non-experimental studies, independent variables are observed variables that may influence a variable of interest, i.e. the dependent variable.
c. A dependent variable is the primary variable of interest in an evaluation; evaluators seek to determine how independent variables are influenced by changes in dependent variables.

Mediators and Moderators

The problem statement of an evaluation should be concise and should identify the key factors (variables) of the study. In identifying the key factors, it is important to understand the differences between moderator and mediator effects (Frazier, Tix, & Barron, 2004).

For evaluation or research studies, more than likely, whatever domain we evaluate/investigate includes research questions of the form: *Does variable X predict or cause variable Y?* In this question, X is an independent variable, whereas Y is the dependent variable. In the case of an evaluation, X is an intervention and Y is the outcome (Chen, 2005). Clearly, questions of this general form are basic to evaluation and research. For example, we examine correlational questions such as "What factors are related to students' use of Internet at home?" as well as causal questions such as "Does a certain intervention (e.g., teachers' use of ICT in school) increase students' use of Internet at home?" (see Figure 10.1). To move beyond the basic questions about direct effects (Figure 10.1A), one might examine the moderator and mediator effects.

Questions involving moderators address "when" or "for whom" a variable most strongly predicts or causes an outcome variable. More specifically, a moderator is a variable that changes the direction or strength of the relation between a predictor and an outcome. Thus, a moderator effect is nothing more than an interaction whereby the effect of one variable depends on the level of another (Frazier et al., 2004). For example, in Figure 10.1B, gender (variable G) is introduced as a moderator of the relation between teachers' ICT use in school and students' use of the Internet at home. If gender is a significant moderator in this case, the intervention of teachers' ICT use in school influences students' Internet use at home more for one gender than for the other. Such interaction effects (i.e., moderators) are important because they are common in evaluation. If moderators are ignored in evaluation studies, participants may be given a treatment that is inappropriate or perhaps even harmful for them. The identification of important moderators of relations between intervention and outcomes denotes the sophistication of an evaluation.

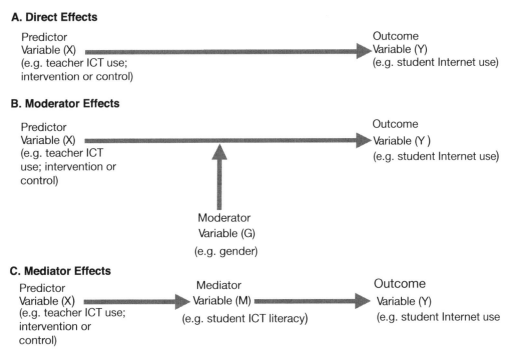

A. Direct Effects

Predictor Variable (X) (e.g. teacher ICT use; intervention or control) → Outcome Variable (Y) (e.g. student Internet use)

B. Moderator Effects

Predictor Variable (X) (e.g. teacher ICT use; intervention or control) → Outcome Variable (Y) (e.g. student Internet use)

Moderator Variable (G) (e.g. gender)

C. Mediator Effects

Predictor Variable (X) (e.g. teacher ICT use; intervention or control) → Mediator Variable (M) (e.g. student ICT literacy) → Outcome Variable (Y) (e.g. student Internet use

FIGURE 10.1 Moderator and Mediator Variables

Moderators address "when" or "for whom" an intervention is more strongly related to an outcome, whereas mediators establish "how" or "why" one variable predicts or causes an outcome variable. More specifically, a mediator is defined as a variable that explains the relation between an intervention and the outcome. In other words, a mediator is the determinant through which an intervention influences the outcome variable (Chen, 2005). In Figure 10.1C, students' ICT literacy (variable M) is introduced as a mediator of the relation between teachers' ICT use in school and students' Internet use at home. If students' ICT literacy is a significant mediator in this case, the result can enable us to focus on the effective components of treatments and remove the ineffective components as well as to build and test theory regarding the causal mechanisms responsible for change. Within the context of evaluating teacher interventions (variable X), measuring underlying change mechanisms (e.g., variable M) as well as outcomes (variable Y) inform the mechanisms that are critical for influencing outcomes.

Test Your Understanding

Which of the following descriptions is not correct?

a. Both mediators and moderators affect the relationship between independent and dependent variables.
b. A moderator affects the direction and/or strength of the relation between an independent and a dependent variable.
c. A moderator must be a qualitative variable, such as gender, race and class.
d. A given variable may be said to function as a mediator to the extent that it accounts for the relation between the predictor and the outcome.

Contextual Factors

A contextual variable is a variable that is constant within a group, but that varies by context. For example, in the field of information technology and specifically the study of data sets, a contextual variable is constant within the group and is calculated based on other variables within the group, which may or may not remain constant. In the study of using computers in schools, contextual variables may involve elements such as technology, financial resources, school environments, and school cultures, and how they affect the use of computers in schools.

Owston (2007) studied factors that contribute to the sustainability of innovative classroom use of technology. Using qualitative data analysis application, he mapped the relationships among codes and developed a model that helps examine why teachers are likely to sustain innovative pedagogical practices using technology. He argued that pedagogical innovation is shaped by a complex interaction of the innovation with contextual factors such as school and school district policy, leadership, cultural norms and values, teacher attitudes and skills, and student characteristics.

In a study of business systems, Anderson and Young (1999) investigated associations between evaluations of activity-based costing systems, contextual factors, and factors related to a specific system's implementation process using interview. Survey data from 21 field research sites of two firms were collected. The study examined the significance of direct associations between 12 contextual factors including individual and organizational factors. Four variables were hypothesized to influence individuals' evaluations of the system. Eight organizational contextual factors were hypothesized to influence evaluations of the system and management involvement in the implementation process. That study focused on organizational factors that were local as a result of different products, processes and people at different sites.

Pintrich, Marx and Boyle (1993) presented an analysis of a conceptual change model for describing student learning by applying research on student motivation to the process of conceptual change. Four general motivational constructs (goals, values, self-efficacy and control beliefs) were suggested as potential mediators of the process of conceptual change. They also argued that the features of the classroom context were important moderators of the relationship between student motivation and cognition. The classroom contextual factors included (a) task structures, (b) authority structures, (c) evaluation structures, (d) classroom management, (e) teacher modeling, and (f) teacher scaffolding.

To sum up, there are a number of points worth reiterating. A contextual variable varies by context, and it may influence the implementation process and outcomes. Contextual factors may connect to individual, organizational or other aspects. In some cases, contextual factors are considered as moderators.

Learning Activities

A cluster of 12 special schools in a city, serving students with different kinds of special needs, has decided to initiate a project to develop an e-learning platform to (a) meet the needs of diverse students, (b) give teachers flexible access to information and pedagogical resources, and (c) help the principals to manage their schools.

If you were asked to evaluate this development project, what are the possible independent variables, outcome variables, mediators, moderators and contextual factors you would consider?

Links

Mediator. (n.d.). In Wikipedia. Retrieved from https://en.wikipedia.org/wiki/Mediator

Moderator. (n.d.). In Wikipedia. Retrieved from https://en.wikipedia.org/wiki/Moderator

References

Anderson, S. W. & Young, S. M. (1999). The impact of contextual and process factors on the evaluation of activity-based costing systems. *Accounting, Organizations and Society, 24*, 525–559.

Chen, H. T. (2005). Theory-driven evaluation. In S. Mathison (Ed.), *Encyclopedia of evaluation* (pp. 415–419). Thousand Oaks, CA: Sage.

Fitzpatrick, J. L., Sanders, J. R., & Worthen, B. R. (2011). *Program evaluation: Alternative approaches and practical guidelines* (4th ed.). Upper Saddle River, NJ: Pearson Education.

Frazier, P. A., Tix, A. P., & Barron, K. E. (2004). Testing moderator and mediator effects in counseling psychology research, *Journal of Counseling Psychology, 51*(1), 115–134.

Owston, R. (2007). Contextual factors that sustain innovative pedagogical practice using technology: An international study. *Journal of Educational Change, 8*(1), 61–77.

Owston, R. (2008). Models and methods for evaluation. In J. M. Spector, M. D. Merrill, J. J. G. van Merriënboer, & M. P. Driscoll (Eds.) *Handbook of research on educational communications and technology* (3rd ed.; pp. 605–617). New York: Routledge.

Pintrich, P. R., Marx, R. W., & Boyle, R. A. (1993). Beyond cold conceptual change: The role of motivational beliefs and classroom contextual factors in the process of conceptual change. *Review of Educational Research, 63*(2), 167–199.

Additional Resources

Hamilton, J., & Feldman, J. (2014). Planning a program evaluation: Matching methodology to program status. In J. M. Spector, M. D. Merrill, J. Elen, & M. J. Bishop (Eds.), *Handbook of research on educational communications and technology* (4th ed., pp. 249–256). New York: Springer.

Kaufman, R. (1988). Preparing Useful Performance Indicators. *Training and Development Journal, 42*(9), 80–83.

Kaufman, R., Keller, J., & Watkins, R. (1996). What works and what doesn't: Evaluation beyond Kirkpatrick. *Performance+ Instruction, 35*(2), 8–12.

McLaughlin, J. A., & Jordan, G.B. (2010), Using logic models. In J. S. Wholey, H. P. Hatry & K. E. Newcomer (Eds.), *Handbook of practical program evaluation*, (3rd ed.; pp 62–87). Hoboken,, NJ: John Wiley & Sons.

Mertens, D. M., & Wilson, A. T. (2012). *Program evaluation theory and practice: A comprehensive guide.* New York: Guilford Press.

Oppenheim, A. N. (1992). *Questionnaire design and attitude measurement.* London: Pinter Publishers.

Petrosino, A. (2000). Answering the why question in evaluation: The causal-model approach. *Canadian Journal of Program Evaluation, 15*(1), 1–24.

Portenoy, R. K., Thaler, H. T., Kornblith, A. B., Lepore, J. M., Friedlander-Klar, H., Kiyasu, E., Sobel, K., Coyle, N., Kemeny, N., Norton, L., & Scher, H. (1994). The Memorial Symptom Assessment Scale: An instrument for the evaluation of symptom prevalence, characteristics and distress. *European Journal of Cancer, 30*(9), 1326–1336.

Rogers, P. J. (2007). Theory-based evaluation: Reflections ten years on. In S. Mathison (Ed.), *Enduring issues in evaluation: The 20th anniversary of the collaboration between NDE and AEA.* New directions for evaluation. Vol. 114 (pp. 63–67). San Francisco, CA: Jossey-Bass Publishers and the American Evaluation Association.

Rogers, P. J., Petrosino, A., Huebner, T. A., & Hacsi, T. A. (2000). Program theory evaluation: Practice, promise, and problems. *New directions for evaluation, 2000*(87), 5–13.

Rooney, J. J., & Heuvel, L. N. V. (2004). Root cause analysis for beginners, *Quality Progress*, July 2004, 45–53.

Spector, J. M. (2014). Program and project evaluation. In J. M. Spector, M. D. Merrill, J. Elen, & M. J. Bishop (Eds.). *Handbook of research on educational communications and technology* (4th ed.; pp. 195–201). New York: Springer.

Weiss, C. H. (1972). *Evaluation research. Methods for assessing program effectiveness.* Englewood Cliffs, NJ: Prentice-Hall.

Weiss, C. H. (1997). Theory-based evaluation: Past, present, and future. *New Directions for Evaluation, 76*, 41–55.

Wiersma, W. (1995). *Research methods in education* (6th ed.). Boston, MA: Allyn & Bacon.

Zikmund, W. (1997). *Business research methods* (5th ed.). Orlando, FL: Harcourt College.

part three

LOGIC MODELS AND IMPLEMENTATIONS

eleven
Interventions and Implementation Plans

The surest way to corrupt a youth is to instruct him to hold in higher esteem those who think alike than those who think differently.

(from Friedrich Nietzsche's The Dawn, *1881*)

Educational projects, programs, products, practices and policies have in common the intention of transforming an undesirable (problematic) situation into a desirable (unproblematic) situation. In essence, the intention is to *change* a particular state of affairs (call it 'A') into a different state of affairs (call it 'B'). To facilitate the desired change from A to B, an intervention is planned and implemented. The intervention (i.e., a project, program, program, practice or policy) is intended to facilitate, support or even cause the desired change. A question that should be asked and answered early in the effort is why one should believe that the proposed intervention will bring about (or help bring about) the desired change. In other words, there is a need to develop what we (and others) are calling a theory of change for that particular situation (Chen, 2005). The European Commission calls this aspect of the methodology associated with an effort the *intervention logic* (see www.ec.europa.eu/europeaid/evaluation/methodology/methods/mth_log_en.htm).

A theory of change can be considered the logic behind the intervention. Figure 11.1 depicts the general logic that applies to an educational intervention. A theory of change should explain how and why a problematic situation will be changed by an intervention into a desired or less problematic situation.

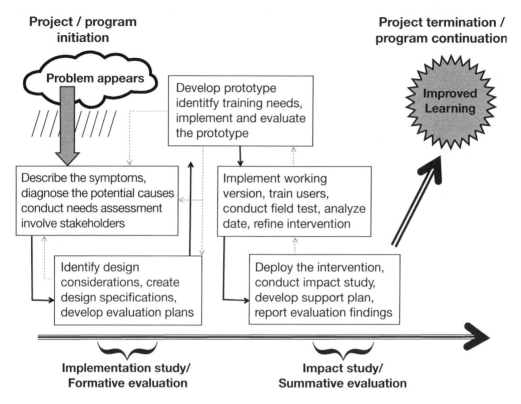

Project / program initiation

Problem appears

Develop prototype
identitfy training needs,
implement and evaluate
the prototype

Project termination / program continuation

Improved Learning

Describe the symptoms,
diagnose the potential causes
conduct needs assessment
involve stakeholders

Implement working
version, train users,
conduct field test, analyze
date, refine intervention

Identify design
considerations, create
design specifications,
develop evaluation plans

Deploy the intervention,
conduct impact study,
develop support plan,
report evaluation findings

**Implementation study/
Formative evaluation**

**Impact study/
Summative evaluation**

FIGURE 11.1 The Logic of Change

Interventions

Educational interventions take many forms and exist at a variety of levels. At the activity level with an individual learner, an intervention might take the form of a teacher helping a student understand how to solve a particular problem or why an attempted solution was not correct. At the course level, an intervention might take the form of a course redesign, moving from a lecture-based approach to an interactive simulation-based approach. At an institutional level, an intervention might take the form of standards and procedures pertaining to reporting or changing grades. At the state or national level, an intervention might take the form of policies and legislation to guide local and regional efforts (see www2.ed.gov/policy/landing.jhtml?src=ft for an elaboration in the context of the USA). The United Nations Educational, Scientific and Cultural Organization (UNESCO) has many resources and guidelines for all aspects of education at all levels, including research and evaluation (see www.en.unesco.org/themes/education-21st-century).

Examples of the various types of educational interventions in which technology plays a key role can also be found at nearly every level. For example, a software application for mobile devices to support learning a foreign language is an intervention product that might be used at multiple levels (e.g., at the individual activity level, lesson level, and/or course level). At the practice level, an institution might require that all publications be completed using a particular reference style and product (e.g., EndNote or RefWorks) that can be automatically transformed into another reference style. An institution may want to standardize online course offerings requiring open source licensing and using one learning management system and issue a policy expressing those requirements and a mandate requiring that current courses not using that system be brought into compliance within a specified period of time. As previously discussed, educational technology projects and programs are the most common types of things that are evaluated and many examples can be found.

When planning an intervention, it is standard practice to document the current situation and the desired situation, including the reasons being put forth as the motivation for a change. In very general terms, this involves specifying a *gap* between what exists and what is desired. Gap analysis is a well-established practice in project management (Davis, Misra, & van Auken, 2002; Harvey & Kamvounias, 2007). Once a difference between a current and desired state of affairs has been established, it is likely that one or more approaches for bridging the gap will become evident. For each of these approaches, or the nature of the gap itself, one can then conduct a review of what is known about the gap or the approach being considered. Typical sources include research and development publications, trade journals, and best practices reported in a number of places.

An investigation of these sources can be used to establish what is known and what is not known with regard to the gap or the approach being considered. Figure 11.2 depicts

source construct	Research & Development Literature	Practitioner & Trade Literature	Best Practices Literature
Category 1			
Category 2			
Category 3			
Category 4			
Category 5			

FIGURE 11.2 A Gap Analysis Matrix Template

one way to represent this information in the form of a gap analysis matrix. The categories in Figure 11.2 could correspond to alternative solution approaches, or they could correspond to specific factors influencing the gap in question. For example, if the problematic situation is that students are not doing the homework necessary to develop required problem solving skills, then a number of alternative approaches might be investigated, including (a) a flipped classroom, (b) the use of partially worked examples, (c) assigning grades for homework turned in on time, (d) length of in class lectures, (e) time for questions and individual support in class, and so on.

On the other hand, if the solution that is being pursued is a flipped classroom, then the categories might represent different aspects or factors involved in flipping the classroom, such as (a) length of outside class assignment, (b) modality of the outside assignment (e.g., video, audio, text, etc.), (c) source of the outside assignment (e.g., Internet, textbook, handheld device, etc.), (d) time available for individual and small group work in class, (e) student self-regulation skills, and so on. Knowing what works and when and with whom is important when selecting a solution approach. One place to start elaborating a gap analysis matrix is the What Works Clearinghouse (see the What Works Clearinghouse of the US Institute of Education Sciences—www.ies.ed.gov/ncee/wwc/).

Test Your Understanding

With regard to the possibility of introducing a flipped classroom approach to a lesson or unit of instruction, answer the following and discuss with classmates:

1. A good reason to introduce a flipped classroom approach for a lesson is that:

   a. it will free up time for the teacher to grade papers while students work on problems in class;
   b. it will require students to do the outside assignment;
   c. it will provide more time in the classroom for the teacher to provide individual feedback to students working on problems; and
   d. it will shift the burden for enforcing doing outside assignments from the teacher to the parents.

2. Using What Works Clearinghouse: Publications & Products (see www.ies.ed.gov/ncee/wwc/Publications_Reviews.aspx?f=All+Publication+and+Product+Types%2c1%3b), indicate how many resources and which ones for the following search terms when searching all topics and publication/production types:

   a. flipped classroom
   b. evaluation
   c. collaborative learning
   d. TPACK
   e. Educational technology

Theory of Change

A theory of change (a.k.a. the intervention logic) explains how the design, development and deployment of an intervention, including all associated activities (e.g., needs assessment, requirements analysis, training, etc.) will bring about the desired results.

A systems IPO perspective involving *inputs* (current states or situations), *processes* (practices, policies, approaches, methods, environments, activities, etc.), and *outputs* (desired states such as improved learning outcomes, deeper understanding, more efficient educational systems, etc.) provides one way to conceptualize and represent a theory of change. A theory of change should explain why the proposed means of transforming an existing state of affairs into a desired state of affairs is reasonable and likely to succeed. Moreover, a theory should explain how that transformation is going to take place in terms of stages, phases, steps, and so on. Resources (time, effort and funds) are about to be committed to a process intended to improve a problematic or undesirable situation. Why should one believe that the proposed intervention will achieve the desired outcomes? Answering this question involves elaborating a theory of change. The answer typically involves a review and analysis of prior research, development and practice along with a general theory that supports the evidence gathered for a particular approach or solution.

Linking evidence and best practices with examples and theoretical foundations is often an effective way to develop a theory of change. A theory of change can then be used to enlist the support required to carry out the proposed intervention or change. For example, suppose one has learned that American students in a required lower division college history course seem disinterested in the history of the Napoleonic wars in Europe, and these students tend to perform poorly on simple declarative knowledge tests involving the history of western Europe in the first part of the nineteenth century. When asked, students report spending very little time on reading and studying related resources involved in that portion of the course. A review of the research on learning in history and other subjects suggests that the time that students spend on a learning task tends to be highly correlated with learning outcomes (Kidron & Lindsay, 2014). This leads to the possibility of creating an activity that will be likely to involve more time on learning-related tasks and therefore result in improved learning. A review of the research on motivation suggests that a game, especially one with a competitive aspect, can be addictive and engaging, causing someone to spend time playing the game (Garris, Ahlers, & Driskell, 2002). Suppose one devises a game involving identifying key battles and leaders in that historical era. The game could be played after reading the textbook or with the textbook open while playing the game. It could be a timed game with each correctly identified item yielding a certain number of points and an incorrectly identified item resulting in points deducted. At the end of the game playing period, the person with the highest score receives some kind of reward or special recognition. The theory of change involved in such an effort might be depicted as in Figure 11.3.

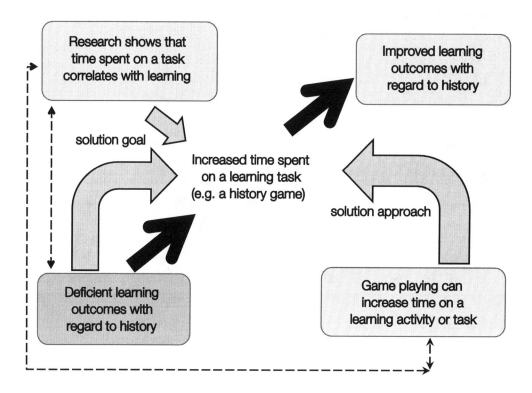

FIGURE 11.3 Simple Theory of Change Example

Test Your Understanding

1. Which of the following statements about a theory of change is reasonable:

   a. The theory of change was proposed by Heraclitus to explain why things are never what they appear to be.
   b. A theory of change is also known as the logic of an intervention.
   c. The theory of change explains how a problematic situation can be expected to be transformed into a less problematic situation.
   d. A theory of change can be represented visually as well as in text.
   e. The theory of change for an intervention refers to those aspects of the situation that will be changed and those that will not be changed.

2. Indicate in text or visually a theory of change that might be appropriate for using a flipped classroom approach in a particular situation.

A Representative Educational Technology Challenge

Consider again the situation in which a large residential institution has decided to begin offering e-learning programs and MOOCs in order to increase enrollments and reach students who are not able to engage in a full-time residential college education. The first program to be involved in this five-year plan is a master's level program in educational leadership that targets K-12 school principals and school district supervisors who will be working full-time. What might be involved in developing a theory of change or intervention logic for this case?

Learning Activities

1. Identify and describe the key factors or constructs that you would consider to be categories to be investigated as part of a review of the research and development literature for this case.
2. Specify a logical chain of reasoning that leads from the current situation to a more desirable situation.

Links

Theory of Change: Technical Papers—a series of papers to support development of theories of changes based on practice in the field—see www.actknowledge.org/resources/documents/ToC-Tech-Papers.pdf

US Department of Education: Laws & Guidance—see www2.ed.gov/policy/landing.jhtml?src=ft

The What Works Clearinghouse of the US Institute of Education Sciences—see www.ies.ed.gov/ncee/wwc/

Other Resources

The US Department of Education's Policies Website—see www.det.wa.edu.au/policies/detcms/portal/

Article by Lee, Strong, Kahn & Wang entitled "AIMQ: A Methodology for Information Quality Assessment" published in 2002 in *Information & Management, 40*(2), 133–146—see www.sciencedirect.com/science/article/pii/S0378720602000435

The European Commission Website for Education and Training—see www.ec.europa.eu/education/policy/strategic-framework/indicators-benchmarks_en.htm

The United Nations Educational, Scientific and Cultural Organization (UNESCO) Website for Education in Asia and the Pacific—see www.unesco.org/new/en/education/worldwide/education-regions/asia-and-the-pacific/

References

Chen, H.-T. (2005). Theory-driven evaluation. In S. Mathison (Ed.), *Encyclopedia of evaluation* (pp. 415–419). Thousand Oaks, CA: Sage. Retrieved from www.srmo.sagepub.com/view/encyclopedia-of-evaluation/n542.xml

Davis, R., Misra, S., & van Auken, S. (2002). A gap analysis approach to marketing curriculum assessment: A study of skills and knowledge. *Journal of Marketing Education, 24*(3), 218–224. Retrieved from www.jmd.sagepub.com/content/24/3/218.short

Garris, R., Ahlers, R., & Driskell, J. E. (2002). Games, motivation, and learning: A research and practice model. *Simulation & Gaming, 33*(4), 441–467.

Harvey, A., & Kamvounias, P. (2007). Bridging the implementation gap: A teacher-as-learner approach to teaching and learning policy. *Higher Education Research & Development, 27*(1), 31–41.

Kidron, Y., & Lindsay, J. (2014). *The effects of increased learning time on student academic and non-academic outcomes: Findings from a meta-analytic review* (REL 2014–2015). Washington, DC: US Department of Education, Institute of Education Sciences. Retrieved from www.ies.ed.gov/ncee/edlabs/projects/project.asp?projectID=373

Additional Resource

Anderson, L. W., & Postlethwaite, T. N. (2007). *Program evaluation: Large-scale and small-scale studies.* Brussels: The International Academy of Education and the International Institute for Education. Retrieved from www.unesdoc.unesco.org/images/0018/001817/181752e.pdf

twelve
Developing a
Logic Model

Change is vital . . . improvement the logical form of change.
(James Cash Penny)

In modern architecture, Louis Sullivan (1924) created and elaborated the notion that form should follow function—the notion that the shape (i.e., the physical form) of a building should be based primarily on its intended purpose and use (i.e., its function). Likewise, in instructional design, a widely accepted general principle is that the purpose (e.g., intended learning outcome) and the content to be learned should be clearly aligned (Richey, Klein, & Tracey, 2011). As previously argued, one thing that educational projects, programs, products, practice and policy share is the intention of improving learning, performance and/or instruction. In the previous chapter, this notion was presented as a logical chain linking (a) a current problem or situation, (b) a desire or goal to improve the situation, (c) what is known about factors influencing such a situation, and (d) a proposed intervention or solution. In a sense, the intervention can be considered the content and the desired situation the goal or purpose. Form (e.g., the intervention and associated training and support) follows function (e.g., the purpose or intended outcomes).

A logic model is a tool used by evaluators to depict the logical connections that connect a current state of affairs, what is known about such situations, an intervention or proposed solution, and a desired state of affairs. In other words, a logic model is useful in visually representing the form of an educational effort (the conceptual substance of a solution) and the function (the intended purpose) of that effort. The architectural analog was used because some instructional design scholars have used the better known domain of architecture to elaborate instructional design (see Gibbons, 2014; Sweller, van Merriënboer & Paas, 1998).

Logic Models

When planning and implementing educational interventions, it is useful and sometimes required to have a visual representation—called a logic model herein—to accompany text explaining the effort (the nature of the situation, why a particular solution was selected, how that solution will be implemented, and the specific outcomes expected to result from the effort (see Figure 12.1).

An appropriately detailed logic model can inform an evaluation effort as well as guide research. As indicated in Part I, the questions of concern for an evaluator are whether and to what extent an intervention, technology, learning environment, teaching practice, educational policy or product achieved the intended aims (this is the focus of an impact study or summative evaluation), and why the effort succeeded to the extent it did and/or why it fell short in some way (typically this can be answered through the results of a fidelity of implementation study or other kind of formative evaluation). As a consequence, there are two kinds of studies associated with an evaluation: (a) a fidelity of implementation study, which is a kind of formative evaluation conducted to help keep the effort on track to succeed (but also used to explain the results of an impact study),

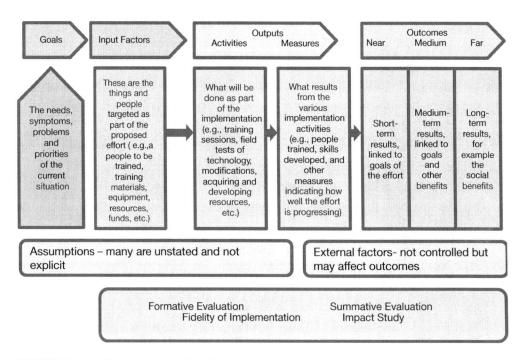

FIGURE 12.1 A Generic Logic Model

Source: See www.blogs.oregonstate.edu/programevaluation/files/2010/12/logicmodel.jpg.

and (b) an impact study, which is a form of summative evaluation that indicates the extent the effort succeeded in attaining intended goals and objectives (see Figure 12.1).

A logic model can be used to explain the differences in these two kinds of research and evaluation studies and to show how what is being designed, developed and deployed links the problem situation with the desired outcomes. That is to say that a logic model is a visual representation of a theory of change (see the previous chapter). A logic model is a visual representation of (a) a problematic situation and the associated underlying problem, (b) implementation of an intervention intended to resolve the problematic situation, and (c) the desired outcomes and benefits of the intervention if it is successful.

In summary, a theory of change explains why and how an effort should lead from a problematic situation to desired outcomes; the logic model is a visual representation of the theory of change. A fidelity of implementation study is a structured formative evaluation of various design, development and deployment efforts that are conducted to identify problem areas requiring attention and eventually used to explain the degree of success (as in high, medium, low, or superior, adequate or marginal) of those efforts. A fidelity of implementation study typically focuses on such things as adherence to the design specifications, initial tryouts and results, modifications along the way, training, professional development, quality assurance and institutional support. Having the data of a fidelity of an implementation study is useful in explaining why and to what extent the effort was successful.

The W. K. Kellogg Foundation (2004) published a comprehensive discussion of logic models and a guide for logic model development. Additional resources pertaining to logic models can be found in the Links and Resources section at the end of this chapter (see also www.smartgivers.org/uploads/logicmodelguidepdf.pdf).

Test Your Understanding

1. Explain the difference between outputs and outcomes in a logic model.
2. Which of the following pertain to a fidelity of implementation study:

    a. a kind of summative evaluation;

    b. used to help keep an effort progressing towards intended goals;

    c. used to identify potential problems in an implementation;

    d. used to explain the extent to which outcomes were achieved; or

    e. a kind of formative evaluation.

3. Which of the following pertain to an impact study:

    a. a kind of summative evaluation;

    b. reports the extent to which an effort achieved intended outcomes;

    c. provides evidence linking the initial situation and goals to the actual outcomes;

    d. focuses on the activities and immediate outputs of those activities; or

    e. a kind of formative evaluation.

Developing a Logic Model

Each of the things that are the focus of an evaluation (project, program, product, practice or policy) are likely to change as the associated planning and implementation evolve. This means that a theory of change and the logic model are subject to modification as the effort progresses. Hopefully, the basic framework of the plan represented by the theory of change and logic model will remain relatively intact. However, many of the activities in the Outputs column of the logic model may yield results that create a need to modify various aspects of the effort. For example, tryouts of an initial interface associated with a product may reveal a need to make changes in the interface. With regard to a project or a program, it often happens that tryouts with an initial group of users reveal a need for more training or training of a different kind prior to widespread deployment. In short, a logic model should be regarded as a flexible guide rather than a rigid framework for the effort.

Once the general flow from a problem specification to an initial solution design are linked to the desired outcomes, a framework for representing the logic can be selected and then elaborated, usually in concert with the team involved in the effort. The generic logic model depicted in Figure 12.1 is one of many possible representations. Others can be found in the Links section at the end of this chapter.

The logic model, like the theory of change, should be constructed based on facts about the problem or situation (vetted with a representative group and revisited with the planning/implementation team), a clear and specific statement of the goals of the effort, and a shared understanding of what prior efforts and the relevant research and development suggest are likely to be key concerns and likely solution approaches.

It should be obvious that the theory of change and the logic model are typically developed together, although the logic model may depict more detail about specific aspects of the development than might be included in the theory of change. In general, a first version of the theory of change guides the development of the logic model, both of which might be modified prior to settling on final versions. As the team elaborates the logic model, constraints created by time, resources and other factors should be considered so that what is developed to guide the effort represents a realistic and feasible depiction of how the effort will proceed from start to finish.

As previously noted, as the effort proceeds, it may be necessary to make modifications to various aspects and adjust the logic model accordingly. If the theory of change has been elaborated at an appropriate level, it is less likely that changes in the theory of change will be necessary, but such changes are possible. When changes are made to the logic model, those changes should be made known to all of the involved parties, including users, administrators and funding agencies. In the case of funded efforts, proposed changes might need to be approved by the funding agency; in such cases, it is helpful to have a rationale and evidence supporting the need for each specific change proposed. If research involving human subjects is involved, it might also be necessary to have an approved amendment to the human subjects approval form that would have been required at the initiation of the effort.

Many evaluation efforts are subject to human subjects approval because those conducting the effort might want to publish results. Both formative and summative evaluations are in general publishable in academic, professional and research venues. In fact, some funding agencies require a publication plan to be submitted along with the proposal. As a result, human subjects approval should be sought in advance if there is even a slight possibility for a publication. Moreover, it is important to publish the results of fidelity of implementation and impact studies, as such publications serve to advance professional practice and inform others of what works (or does not work), when, to what extent and why.

A Representative Educational Technology Challenge

Consider once again the situation in which a large residential institution has decided to begin offering e-learning programs and MOOCs in order to increase enrollments and reach students who are not able to engage in a full-time residential college education. The first program to be involved in this five-year plan is a master's level program in educational leadership that targets K-12 school principals and school district supervisors, who will be working full-time. Following that initial effort, the use of MOOCs to support lower-division enrollment required courses is planned. Develop a logic model and a theory of change to reflect how this expanded effort might be organized and evaluated.

Learning Activities

Develop a logic model and a theory of change to reflect how a project, program, product, practice or policy with which you are or might be involved is or could be organized and evaluated.

Links

W. K. Kellogg Foundation Logic Model Development Guide—see www.smartgivers.org/uploads/logicmodel guidepdf.pdf

Pell Institute Guide to Creating a Logic Model—see www.toolkit.pellinstitute.org/evaluation-guide/plan-budget/use-a-logic-model-in-evaluation/

TidyForm logic model templates—see www.tidyform.com/logic-model-template.html

University of Wisconsin—Extension Website for Program Development and Evaluation—see www.uwex.edu/ces/pdande/evaluation/evallogicmodel.html

Yahoo search results for free logic model templates—see https://images.search.yahoo.com/yhs/search;_ylt=A86.JyAOH6lVZjIA9IknnIlQ;_ylu=X3oDMTEzODltNzAxBGNvbG8DZ3ExBHBvcwMxBHZ0aWQDRkZHRTAxXzEEc2VjA3Nj?p=Free+Logic+Model+Templates&fr=yhs-mozilla-001&hspart=mozilla&hsimp=yhs-001

Other Resources

The Pell Institute's Evaluation Toolkit—see www.toolkit.pellinstitute.org/evaluation-guide/plan-budget/using-a-logic-model/ for a discussion of using a logic model

The ActKnowledge.Org Website for social change—see www.actknowledge.org/

United Way Guide to Developing an Outcome Logic Model and Measurement Plan—see www.yourunitedway.org/sites/uwaygrp.oneeach.org/files/Guide_for_Logic_Models_and_Measurements.pdf

References

Gibbons, A. S. (2014). *An architectural approach to instructional design*. New York: Routledge.

Richey, R. C., Klein, J. D., & Tracey, M. W. (2011). *The instructional design knowledge base: Theory, research and practice*. New York: Routledge.

Sullivan, L. H. (1924). *Autobiography of an idea*. New York: Press of the American Institute of Architectures.

Sweller, J., van Merriënboer, J. J. G., & Paas, F. G. W. C. (1998), Cognitive architecture and instructional design. *Educational Psychology Review, 10*(3), 251–296.

W. K. Kellogg Foundation (2004). *Using logic models to bring together planning, evaluation, and action: Logic model development guide*. Battle Creek, MI: W. K. Kellogg Foundation. Retrieved from www.smartgivers.org/uploads/logicmodelguidepdf.pdf

Additional Resource

Taplin, D. H., Clark, H., Collins, E., & Colby, D. C. (2013). *Theory of change: Technical papers*. New York: ActKnowledge.

thirteen
Identifying Indicators and Measurements

There are two possible outcomes: If the result confirms the hypothesis, then you've made a measurement. If the result is contrary to the hypothesis, then you've made a discovery.
(Enrico Fermi)

The reason that the title of this chapter is 'indicators and measurements' is to emphasize the notion that *evidence* is fundamental (especially systematically gathered and carefully analyzed evidence), but not all evidence comes in the form of numerical or quantifiable measurements. Since the word 'measurement' is typically associated with numerical measures such as length, distance, time, test score and such, the notion pursued herein is that both numerical measurements and other systematically gathered indicators are relevant to making a determination with regard to progress toward goals and overall impact of an effort. Hereafter, the term 'measurement' will be used to include both numerical and non-numerical measurements consistent with common practice in social science (see www.socialresearchmethods.net/kb/measure.php).

Given the broad interpretation of measurement adopted herein, the guiding belief of this chapter and of evaluation in general is that one gets what one measures. This is known as the WYMIWYG (pronounced 'whim-ee-whig') principle—what you measure is what you get (Spector, 2012, 2015). Unless you have reliable indicators for progress towards goals or outcomes, one cannot make claims with regard to having made progress or attained goals. Without indicators, one does not know what one has. More importantly, an effort will tend to make every effort possible to attain indicated goals, so it is important to set high but achievable goals and then see how close to those goals the effort has come.

Output Measures

Just as Tennyson's (1995) ISD model (Figure 2.1) suggests that situation evaluation applies to each activity and process involved in designing, developing and deploying instruction, there can and should be an evaluation of each activity represented in the outputs column of a logic model. Some of these activities can be measured using numerical measurements. For example, the number and percentage of teachers trained in using a new technology can be easily determined, as can the length of time involved in the training, and perhaps the degree to which targeted knowledge and skills were attained.

In some cases a numerical indicator will suggest a problem. It may happen that many teachers fail to complete the training or perform poorly on a post-training exercise. To understand why, interviews may be conducted that can lead the team back to design or development to address the issue. Such non-numerical indicators are often a critical part of a fidelity of implementation study (discussed in more detail in a subsequent chapter).

Given the previous suggestion to aim high with regard to goals, when implementing a solution in a school context, this might lead one to hope that all teachers could be trained to master the use of a new technology. However, that is an unlikely result, although as a target it might be acceptable. The point here is to develop appropriate output measures for each activity elaborated in the logic model. It is likely that there will be both numerical and non-numerical indicators for many activities. This, in fact, is desirable, as having both kinds of indicators allows one to develop confidence in and explain the results of an activity or process involved in the implementation of an effort.

While the activities and processes involved in implementing an effort vary quite a bit, it is difficult to offer a general set of guidelines. Rather, once the activities and processes are identified, it is appropriate to consider each one individually and determine how best the result of that activity or process can be measured. In some cases, a survey of those involved might be used. In such a case, a survey instrument might need to be developed and tested. In other cases, interviews with those involved might be more appropriate, in which case an interview might be established to guide a structured or semi-structured interview. In other cases, a measure of time required or number of attempts used to find an acceptable solution might be an appropriate indicator.

In cases involving numerical measurements, the data might be ordinal, such as responses to a question about how well the technology performed—well, adequately, poorly, etc. Some data might be nominal, such as the demographic characteristics of those involved. It could happen, for instance, that younger teachers react differently to a technology than older teachers; having access to such nominal data as age and education level can add substance to a fidelity of implementation study and suggest refinements in the implementation so that better results for all are attained.

In cases involving non-numerical measurements (e.g., analyzing interviews), there is generally an attempt to detect patterns among a variety of responses. Depending on the scale of the effort and the number of persons involved, it might be necessary to develop coding schemes and conduct inter-rater reliability tests to have confidence in how those non-numerical measurements are interpreted.

Ultimately, the point of having output measures is to provide the data required for a fidelity of implementation or other kind of formative evaluation study. The reason for conducting such a study is to identify trouble spots and problems in the implementation that can be addressed and potentially corrected prior to full-scale deployment. This is consistent with the notion that the primary responsibility of an evaluator or evaluation team is to help ensure the success of the effort. In addition, having the kind of measurements involved in a formative evaluation can be used to explain the degree to which the outcomes were achieved (i.e., the results of an impact study).

Outcome Measures

The outcomes column of the logic model is often divided into short-, medium- and long-term outcomes. The short-term and medium-term outcomes typically link directly to the goals of the effort or the specific problematic circumstances that prompted the effort. Perhaps the problematic situation is that too many high school students are not graduating on time or are dropping out of school altogether. Then, the short- or medium-term outcomes of the effort are to improve the graduation rate–perhaps with a 5 percent increase in the short term and a 10 percent increase in the long term.

Another example might be that a school has been placed on a poorly performing list due to consistently low student test scores. That situation might prompt an effort aimed at improving test scores and getting the school off the poorly performing list. The short-term and medium-term outcomes might then be linked directly to that goal, again with graduated improvements from the shorter term to the medium term.

One can imagine other cases. There are two points to emphasize at this point. First, the short- and medium-term outcomes should link directly and obviously back to the problem situation and goals of the effort. Second, the associated measurements for short- and medium-term outcome are most often numerical in nature, often involving interval (e.g., test scores) and ratio (e.g., graduation rates) data that are especially well-suited to statistical analysis. That is to say that most impact studies are primarily quantitative in nature, although there can and often are supporting measures involving ordinal and nominal data as well as non-numerical data.

Long-term outcomes are typically associated with the overarching rationale for an effort and often go unmeasured for a variety of reasons (e.g., insufficient time, insufficient funds, fuzziness of the longer term goals, etc.). For example, one reason for wanting to increase graduation rates (measureable as short- and medium-term outcomes) is to increase the quality of productivity of the workforce, or increase the numbers of graduates pursuing post-graduate education in a particular field (e.g., in a STEM-related discipline). The reason to include long-term outcomes is to strengthen the argument for engaging in the effort as it is likely to lead to long-term benefits of interest to the institution or to society. However, it is very often beyond the scope of an effort to measure those longer-term outcomes.

The exception is with regard to a longitudinal study in which the major rationale for the effort is to realize those longer-term outcomes. While such longitudinal studies and efforts are quite valuable and informative, they are all too rare in educational research (in contrast to healthcare research) (White & Arzi, 2005).

Test Your Understanding

1. Describe and give examples of numerical and non-numerical measurements that might be involved in a formative evaluation study.
2. Which of the following are likely output measures?

   a. the number of persons initially trained in a first tryout of a new technology being implemented;
   b. the degree to which overall performance improved as a result of a full-scale implementation of the new technology;
   c. interviews with those involved in an initial tryout;
   d. test scores of students after the new technology has been implemented; or
   e. the percentage of students changing attitudes about careers as a result of the implementation.

3. Which of the following are likely outcome measures?

   a. the number of persons initially trained in a first tryout of a new technology being implemented;
   b. the degree to which overall performance improved as a result of a full-scale implementation of the new technology;
   c. interviews with those involved in an initial tryout;
   d. test scores of students after the new technology has been implemented; or
   e. the percentage of students changing attitudes about careers as a result of the implementation.

A Representative Educational Technology Challenge

Consider a situation in which a medium-sized school district has decided to implement flipped classrooms and personalized learning. The first phase of this four-year effort will be to introduce a flipped classroom approach in half of the 20 elementary schools in the district, beginning with third grade classrooms in the first year, and then fourth grade classrooms in the second year. In the third year, the remaining ten schools will begin, which will allow for improved training and support from the first two years' experience. With the first group, beginning in the third year, the fifth grade classrooms will begin adopting a flipped classroom approach, as will all of the third, fourth and fifth grade classrooms of the second half of the schools. This graduated approach allows for both a comparative analysis as well as for a duration of treatment study. The personalized learning portion of the effort will be undergoing planning only during these years and only be implemented in a follow-on effort (assuming funding allows). The challenge is to develop an evaluation plan for the flipped classroom portion of the effort, including a theory of change and logic model.

Learning Activities

1. Provide a short (no more than 500 words) statement that could serve as a theory of change for such an effort. This statement should proceed from a problem or current situation statement (imagine something realistic) through the planned intervention with a justification and rationale to a desired outcome state.
2. Develop an initial logic model consistent with the theory of change.
3. Elaborate at least one of the outputs including an appropriate measurement.
4. Elaborate a short-term outcome including an appropriate measurement.

Links

William M. K. Trochim's Research Methods Knowledge Base—see www.socialresearchmethods.net/kb/measure.php

Educational Impact Evaluation, SRI International—see www.sri.com/research-development/impact-evaluation

Fidelity of Implementation, the IRIS Center at Vanderbilt University—see www.iris.peabody.vanderbilt.edu/module/fid/

Don Clark's Types of Evaluations in Instructional Design—see www.nwlink.com/~donclark/hrd/isd/types_of_evaluations.html

The University of California at Berkeley's Center for Teaching and Learning—https://teaching.berkeley.edu/formative-evaluations

Other Resources

Center for Public Education—see www.centerforpubliceducation.org/Learn-About/21st-Century/The-21st-century-job.html

Educational Longitudinal Study of 2002, National Center for Education Statistics—see www.nces.ed.gov/surveys/els2002/

References

Spector, J. M. (2012). *Foundations of educational technology: Integrative approaches and interdisciplinary perspectives*. New York: Routledge.

Spector, J. M. (2015). *Foundations of educational technology: Integrative approaches and interdisciplinary perspectives* (2nd ed.). New York: Routledge.

White, R. T., & Arzi, H. J. (2005). Longitudinal studies: Design, validity, practicality, and value. *Research in Science Education, 35*(1), 137–149.

fourteen
Measurement Instrumentation and Protocols

There is nothing like looking, if you want to find something. You certainly usually find something, if you look, but it is not always quite the something you were after.

(J. R. R. Tolkien)

When conducting formative and summative evaluations of projects, programs, products, practices and policy, it is a good idea to treat those evaluations as seriously and as formally as is feasible and reasonable within the constraints of the context in which one is working. If one treats those evaluations as research efforts that could be published in a professional or academic journal, then the guidelines for instrumentation and protocols that apply to research efforts and that are typically reviewed by institutional review boards (IRBs) will apply. Using IRB-approved procedures contributes to reliability and can help ensure success. Moreover, one is then in a position to publish findings. Some journals welcome such evaluation reports because they contribute to the knowledge base in the broad domain of educational technology (Spector, Johnson, & Young, 2014).

From Needs Assessment to Evaluation

As discussed previously, evaluations are generally based on the alignment of the effort with the problem situation and/or goals. Formative evaluations are aimed at helping the effort attain its goals, and summative evaluations are aimed at reporting the extent to which goals have been attained. A critical issue, then, is that developing measures, instruments and protocols for evaluations concerns the specified goals of the effort.

A good starting place for developing measures, instruments and protocols is a needs assessment or training requirements study if one has been conducted and is available to the evaluation team. The reason for this is simple. A needs assessment or training requirements study often involves surveys, interviews and/or focus group discussions with the key people involved with and affected by the effort, which is often a plan to update or replace an existing project, program, product, practice or policy. The findings of a needs assessment study or training requirements analysis are often the driving force behind the planned or ongoing effort to be evaluated. Moreover, the instruments used in a needs assessment or training requirements might well be re-purposed for use in an evaluation study.

A comprehensive treatment of needs assessment and training requirements analysis is beyond the scope of this volume (see McCawley, 2009; Reviere, Berkowitz, Carter & Ferguson, 2008). However, pertinent to measures, instrumentation and protocols is a review of some of the instruments and approaches commonly used (Table 14.1).

While the questions used in the kinds of instruments indicated in Table 14.1 may not have been carefully developed and may lack supporting verification and validation research, they have the advantage of being what was in fact used. Asking the same questions as an effort evolves and is implemented allows the evaluation team to compare findings with the initial data used to motivate the effort.

In addition to these common forms of collecting data in a needs assessment or for an evaluation, another approach can prove useful. Namely, asking those involved to trace the flow of things involved in a process or practice can reveal discrepancies in how those involved think about that process or practice.

One issue to be addressed in needs assessments as well as evaluation studies concerns the representativeness of the persons responding. No single person or group should dominate such studies. All relevant groups should be represented, and a significant

TABLE 14.1 Common Instruments and Approaches

Type of Instrument/Approach	Type of Data	Appropriate Use
Summaries and syntheses of extant data and information	Quantitative (e.g., test scores, graduation rates)	Establishing a baseline point of reference, establishing trends, identifying specific problems
Survey Questionnaires	Quantitative (some qualitative data possible)	Determining perceptions and attitudes about a practice, product, policy, program or process
Interviews	Qualitative	Determining perceived needs, desires, and problem areas
Focus Groups	Qualitative	Identifying areas of consensus with regard to strengths and weaknesses; determining areas where discrepancies and shortfalls exist
Document Reviews	Qualitative and Quantitative	Understanding existing practices, processes, constraints and other environmental factors

number from each group involved should be included in surveys, interviews, focus groups and so on. What one person or group finds objectionable or acceptable may not be viewed the same way by another person or group. Assuring representativeness of respondents and participants is a requirement in research studies, and it is a desirable goal when conducting evaluations (Davern, 2008).

Existing data such as test scores and graduation rates might well provide the basis for an impact study if those were aligned with goals and objectives. Analyzing relevant documents used to support an effort and comparing that analysis and perceptions of those involved with the initial documents reviewed can also provide a useful indication of progress. Moreover, identifying individuals who are resisting a change or who may need additional training and support should be an ongoing concern as a change process proceeds (Ellsworth, 2015; Rogers, 2003).

Validated and Reliable Instruments

A validated instrument is one that has been demonstrated to measure what it was intended to measure. External validity refers to the degree to which findings can be generalized from the responding sample to a larger population (see the previous discussion of representative samples). Content validity refers to appropriateness of the instrument in terms of measuring what one is seeking to determine. Problems often arise when using an instrument to measure perceptions and attitudes, so content validity is an especially important concern for those aspects of an evaluation study.

A reliable instrument is one that consistently measures what it was intended to measure. In the previous discussion, using the same questions in an evaluation instrument that were used in a needs assessment study assumes that the instrument itself is reliable (e.g., without ambiguous questions or questions that might depend on the specific circumstance in or preceding the questionnaire). Using the same raters or coders for open-ended responses can help improve reliability; inter-rater reliability studies can also add confidence in the reliability of instruments that collect data subject to interpretation.

Establishing the validity and reliability of an instrument is not a trivial task, and in many cases constitutes research appropriate for publication or for a graduate thesis or dissertation. As a consequence, it is often advisable to use an instrument that has been established to be valid and reliable. Many university libraries provide assistance and guidelines in finding validated instruments. One can also search the Education Research Information Clearinghouse (see www.eric.ed.gov) or the STEM Learning and Research Center (see www.stelar.edc.org/highlights/evaluation-context-itest-projects).

From Instruments to Instrumentation and Protocols

In addition to having a validated and reliable instrument to use in an evaluation study, it is important to develop a standard protocol for its use. Such a protocol would typically be developed in validation and reliability studies. The instrument itself and the protocols for its proper use constitute instrumentation. Examples of relevant protocols involve such things as what information and instructions will be provided to respondents and in what form and at what time. The same information delivered in the same way should be used each time the instrument is used. Even such simple things as the layout of questions on a survey instrument can influence responses, so those should be followed as published in a validation study. The order of items and time allowed to respond should be standard and form part of an instrumentation protocol. Another example of a protocol involves the introduction provided at the beginning of a focus group discussion. How findings are to be analyzed constitutes part of the use of the instrument and is, therefore, part of the relevant instrumentation.

Changes from protocols established in a validation study should be tested with a small but representative group to ensure that the changes do not diminish the validity of the instrument. In addition, changes in how data are to be analyzed also need to be tested with a small but representative group. Obviously changes to the instrument itself create a need for further validation with a representative group of respondents or participants.

Test Your Understanding

Which of the following are true:

1. When making small changes to a validated instrument, it is not necessary to re-test the use of that instrument with a small but representative group.
2. The instruments used in a needs assessment can be used or inform the instruments to be used in an evaluation study.
3. Evaluation studies are not subject to the same rigors as a research study.
4. Evaluation studies can be published and provide important knowledge for the professional community.
5. Publication of an evaluation study may require having human subjects' approval and clearance from the involved organization or institution.
6. A valid instrument is one that measures what it was supposed to measure.
7. A reliable instrument is one that measures what it was supposed to measure.
8. Coding schemes and methods of analysis are not part of the instrumentation.
9. Evaluation studies involve only qualitative measures and instruments.
10. Impact studies involve only quantitative measures and instruments.

A Representative Educational Technology Challenge

Consider again the situation in which a medium-sized school district has decided to implement flipped classrooms and personalized learning. The first phase of this four-year effort will be to introduce a flipped classroom approach in half of the 20 elementary schools in the district, beginning with third grade classrooms in the first year, and then fourth grade classrooms in the second year. In the third year, the remaining ten schools will begin, which will allow for improved training and support from the first two years' experience. With the first group, beginning in the third year, the fifth grade classrooms will begin adopting a flipped classroom approach, as will all of the third, fourth and fifth grade classrooms of the second half of the schools. This graduated approach allows for both a comparative analysis as well as for a duration of treatment study. The challenge is to develop relevant measures and identify validated and reliable instruments to support the formative and summative evaluation of this effort.

Learning Activities

First identify relevant measures for both a fidelity of implementation study and an impact study. Then identify any validated instruments and association instrumentation that can be used to support the evaluation plan.

Links

Assessment & Evaluation in Higher Education (relevant academic journal)—www.tandfonline.com/loi/caeh20#.VaqDjC5a1vk

Evaluation & Program Planning (relevant academic journal)—see www.journals.elsevier.com/evaluation-and-program-planning/

National Science Foundation—Published Instruments Used by ITEST Projects to Measure Impact—see www.stelar.edc.org/sites/stelar.edc.org/files/data_brief_issue2_0.pdf

Other Resources

California Department of Education, Training and Education Needs Assessment Survey: Final Report—see www.cns.ucdavis.edu/content/research/tena-survey-report-10-26.pdf

Education Research Information Clearinghouse (ERIC)—see www.eric.ed.gov

The National Center for Education Statistics' Site for Needs Assessment—see www.nces.ed.gov/pubs2005/tech_suite/part_2.asp

Office of Migrant Education, Comprehensive Needs Assessment—see www2.ed.gov/admins/lead/account/compneedsassessment.pdf

Peer Education & Evaluation Center, Validated Evaluation Instruments—see www.peer.hdwg.org/sites/default/files/ValidatedEvaluationInstruments.pdf

STEM Learning and Research Center—see www.stelar.edc.org/highlights/evaluation-context-itest-projects

University of North Carolina, School Technology Needs Assessment—see www.serve.org/stna.aspx

University of Washington Health Sciences Library, Measurement Tools/Research Instruments—see www.libguides.hsl.washington.edu/c.php?g=99174&p=641942

References

Davern, M. D. (2008). Representative sample. In P. J. Lavrakas (Ed.), *Encyclopedia of survey research methods* (pp. 721–723). Thousand Oaks, CA: Sage Publications.

Ellsworth, J. B. (2015). *Change agency.* In J. M. Spector (Ed.), *The SAGE encyclopedia of educational technology* (pp. 97–100). Thousand Oaks, CA: Sage Publications.

McCawley, P. F. (2009). *Methods for conducting an educational needs assessment: Guidelines for cooperative extensive system professionals.* Moscow, ID: University of Idaho. Retrieved from www.cals.uidaho.edu/edcomm/pdf/BUL/BUL0870.pdf

Reviere, R., Berkowitz, Carter, C. C., & Ferguson, C. G. (Eds.) (2008). *Needs assessment: A creative and practice guide for social scientists.* New York: Routledge.

Rogers, E. M. (2003). *Diffusion of innovations* (5th ed.). New York: Simon & Schuster.

Spector, J. M., Johnson, T. E., & Young, P. A. (2014). An editorial on research and development in and with educational technology. *Educational Technology Research & Development, 62*(2), 1–12.

fifteen
Fidelity of Implementation Plans

The Universal Underlying Principal of all Stuff (UUPS; pronounced 'oops') is that something has already gone wrong. The first corollary is that mistakes rarely occur in isolation. The second corollary is that resources are rarely adequate to do what one believes should be done. The third corollary is that others generally have better ideas.

(J. M. Spector)

The importance of formative evaluation has been strongly emphasized throughout this volume, along with the claim that helping an effort succeed was a primary responsibility of the evaluator or evaluation team. As depicted in Figure 11.1 and elsewhere, a fidelity of implementation study is one form of formative evaluation. The Institute of Education Sciences typically requires an evaluation plan to accompany a proposal, and part of that evaluation plan should be a fidelity of implementation study (see, for example, www. ies.ed.gov/funding/grantsearch/details.asp?ID=1200). The reason is simple—a promising effort can fail to have the intended impact if not implemented properly. Stated differently, problems with the implementation can detract from achieving the outcomes of a well-conceived and well-designed effort. In the words of Robert Burns (1785), "the best laid plans of mice and men gang aft agley" (i.e., plans often go awry).

Fidelity in this context refers to the degree to which the implementation or effort is consistent with and carefully aligned to the stated goals and objectives of the effort. A fidelity of implementation study is primarily descriptive in nature, describing what is happening or has happened as it pertains to the intended outcomes. This includes design processes, tryouts with selected users, training development, training sessions, and such things that are a critical part of implementation (Dusenbury, Brannigan, Falco, & Hansen, 2003; Ruiz-Primo, 2005).

Dane and Schneider (1988) identify five dimensions of fidelity:

- adherence—the effort is being implemented as planned;
- exposure—participants are involved in some/many/most/all of the efforts components;
- quality—support for the effort from theory, empirical research and best practices;
- responsiveness—the degree to which users are engaged and respond favorably to the effort; and
- differentiation—unique features of the effort that distinguish it from the prior situation and other efforts.

The notion of quality as a focus is particularly significant. Henry Halff (1993) cited three levels of tested an instructional software product; the first of those three levels involved a quality review to ensure that the effort (in this case a technology-based product) was ready for review by potential users. Ross and Morrison (1995) provide an argument that evaluation research, including what is now commonly called a fidelity of implementation study, when properly conducted constitutes an important kind of research.

As should be evident from the above dimensions, there is a great deal of flexibility and a variety of approaches to conducting a fidelity of implementation study. The important factor is that the study should examine aspects of the effort that are or should be linked to the stated goals and objectives. This means that factors that are likely to influence the desired outcomes will be included in such a study. Multiple sources and types of data will typically be collected and analyzed.

Fundamentally, the purpose of a fidelity of implementation study is to identify deviations from the plan and potential problem areas that are likely to inhibit fulfillment of intended outcomes. The findings of a fidelity of implementation study should then be provided to those responsible for the design, development and deployment of the effort so as to make appropriate adjustments that are likely to increase the chances for success. In a multiple year effort, it is desirable to conduct a fidelity of implementation study at least once each year so that appropriate adjustments can be made.

As Ruiz-Primo (2005) notes, an additional reason for fidelity of implementation studies is that successful efforts can then be taken to other contexts because fidelity of implementation studies provide protocols and guidelines that can guide those follow-on efforts. While fidelity of implementation studies are well recognized in healthcare settings, they are now becoming a common requirement for efforts funded in other domains, including education.

Linking Goals, Implementation and Outcomes

A fidelity of implementation study is intended to establish a strong link between stated goals and desired outcomes. An implementation effort typically consists of activities that fall generally into three broad categories: design, development and deployment. A robust fidelity of implementation study will address all three categories, although in many cases an early study will precede deployment, even to small groups, and may well even precede a development effort.

For example, prior to investing heavily in a development, one may decide to create a notional prototype to mimic what the intended effort will be like, and then gather feedback from users on that prototype to guide further refinement of the design and development (Rossett, 2009). When an initial functioning prototype has been developed, this process may be repeated with a small group of users, as refinements to the design are still feasible and affordable in the early stages of development. All such reviews constitute part of a fidelity of implementation study.

As the effort matures, it is often necessary to train users. As a consequence, training materials will need to be developed and tested with representative users prior to full-scale deployment. Recording the development of training materials and the impact of initial training on users is also part of a fidelity of implementation study. In some cases, users may not react well to a prototype not due to any deficiencies between what was planned and what has been developed; rather, some users may still not see the need for a change or appreciate the value of the effort. Such a finding is also significant and should not be brushed aside lightly. Basically, it represents a need for further training and education of users, and perhaps refocusing first on things users are likely to appreciate in the short term, so as to gain their support as the effort evolves.

In summary, major components of a fidelity of implementation study include: (a) the design itself; (b) the perceived benefits of that design with users; (c) reactions to an initial prototype or partial development; (d) training materials; (e) training session details, such as content, length, participation, etc.; (f) reactions to training materials and training sessions; (g) changes made to the design and development; and (h) effects on users. To gather such data, a variety of means are required, ranging from observations, surveys, interviews, focus groups, document reviews and so on.

It should be obvious that conducting fidelity of implementation studies is a complex and challenging enterprise. Evaluators need to be gathering data to answer such questions as: (a) Are the resources gathered to support the effort pertinent and adequate? (b) Are design, development and deployment processes structured so as to ensure a quality effort? (c) Are the activities being conducted in the design, development and deployment of the effort resulting in outputs likely to result in attaining goals?

Threats to Fidelity

Recalling the discussion of a theory of change, the broad claim of an effort is that it will result in specific outcomes. This is close to the notion of causality discussed by many educational researchers and investigated in experimental and quasi-experimental research studies. As such, the same things that can threaten the validity of an experimental study might also threaten the fidelity of implementation. A common distinction in educational research is made between internal and external validity (Cook & Campbell, 1979).

Internal validity refers to the claim that the intervention makes a difference and whether or not there is adequate evidence to support that claim. A number of factors can threaten internal validity, including (a) the maturity of the effort (recall Halff's recommendation to first ensure the quality of that which is being evaluated); (b) the selection of those involved in surveys, interviews, focus groups and tryouts; (c) the protocols involved in the use of instruments; (d) changes in the composition of those involved in using what is being developed, and more.

External validity refers to claims about the generalizability of findings (see the previous discussion about representative samples). For example, if an initial phase involved only third grade teachers and the next phase involves all elementary teachers in a school or district, is there an adequate basis for generalizing from the reactions by and impact on third grade teachers to all elementary teachers?

While planning fidelity of implementation studies, it is advisable to consider analogous research designs (see Arthur, Waring, Coe, & Hedges, 2012; see also www.socialresearch methods.net/kb/desdes.php). See Appendix A for a sample fidelity of implementation plan within the context of a larger evaluation plan.

Test Your Understanding

Answer the following questions as indicated:

1. Explain briefly the role of a quality review in the context of a fidelity of implementation study.
2. Which of the following are relevant aspects to examine and document in a fidelity of implementation study:

   a. the qualifications of the design team;
   b. quality control processes established for design and development;
   c. the perceptions of likely users to early prototypes;
   d. publications in the popular press about such efforts;
   e. how a comparison group is developing without the benefits of that which is being developed; or
   f. research studies involving related efforts and technologies.

A Representative Educational Technology Challenge

Consider once again the situation in which a medium-sized school district has decided to implement flipped classrooms and personalized learning. The first phase of this four-year effort will be to introduce a flipped classroom approach in half of the 20 elementary schools in the district, beginning with third grade classrooms in the first year, and then fourth grade classrooms in the second year. In the third year, the remaining ten schools will begin, which will allow for improved training and support from the first two years' experience. With the first group, beginning in the third year, the fifth grade classrooms will begin adopting a flipped classroom approach, as will all of the third, fourth and fifth grade classrooms of the second half of the schools. This graduated approach allows for both a comparative analysis as well as for a duration of treatment study.

Learning Activities

Develop an initial fidelity of implementation study for this effort indicating what would be investigated with which instruments and how findings might inform a re-design and/or further development of the effort. Identify internal and external factors that might threaten the validity (and fidelity) of the study.

Links

Institute of Education Sciences, Fidelity of Implementation—see www.ies.ed.gov/funding/grantsearch/details.asp?ID=1200

Web Center for Social Science Research Methods: Designing Designs for Research—see www.socialresearchmethods.net/kb/desdes.php

Other Resources

Maria Ruiz-Primo's paper on fidelity of implementation—see www.gwu.edu/~scale-up/documents/AERA-Implementation-Ruiz-Primo.pdf

References

Arthur, J., Waring, M., Coe, R., & Hedges, L. V. (2012). *Research methods & methodologies in education*. Thousand Oaks, CA: Sage Publications.

Burns. R. (1795). To a mouse, on turning up in her nest with the plough. Retrieved from www.poetryfoundation.org/poem/173072

Cook, T. D., & Campbell, D. T. (1979). *Quasi-experimentation: Design and analysis issues for field settings*. Boston, MA: Houghton Mifflin.

Dane, A. V., & Schneider, B. H. (1988). Program integrity and early secondary prevention: Are implementation efforts out of control? *Clinical Psychology Review, 18*(1), 23–45.

Dusenbury, L., Brannigan, R., Falco, M., & Hansen, W. B. (2003). A review of research on fidelity of implementation: Implications for drug abuse prevention in school settings. *Health Education Research, 18*(2), 237–256.

Halff, H. M. (1993). Prospects for automating instructional design. In J. M. Spector, M. C. Polson, & D. J. Muraida (Eds.), *Automating instructional design: Concepts and issues* (pp. 67–131). Englewood Cliffs, NJ: Educational Technology Publications.

Ross, S. M., & Morrison, G. R. (1995). Evaluation as a tool for research and development: Issues and trends in its applications in educational technology. In R. D. Tennyson, & A. E. Barron (Eds.), *Automating instructional design: Computer-based development and delivery tools* (pp. 491–522). New York: Springer.

Rossett, A. (2009). *First things fast: A handbook for performance analysis* (2nd ed.). San Francisco, CA: John Wiley & Sons.

Ruiz-Primo, M. A. (2005, April). A multi-method and multi-source approach for studying fidelity of implementation. Paper presented at the AERA Annual Meeting, Montreal, Canada, April 14, 2005.

part four

TRANSLATING PLANS INTO ACTIONS

Chapters 16–20 in this part of the book include elaborations for representative examples of a project, a program, a product, a practice and a policy.

The representative examples are:

- project—a flipped classroom project for an elementary school;
- program—a new online master's degree program in sports management;
- product—a new learning management system (college level);
- practice—small learning groups that cut across middle school grades; and
- policy—a bring-your-own-device (BYOD) policy for a school district.

Chapter 20 focuses specifically on policy. Chapter 21 cuts across these target categories and focuses on documenting, reporting and publishing. Consistent with the notion that publishing evaluation outcomes contribute to the progressive development of the field of educational technology evaluation, particular emphasis has been placed on evaluation in this volume.

sixteen
Milestones for Effective Technology Integration

The Tortoise says to Achilles: "And so you see, in each moment you must be catching up the distance between us, and yet I—at the same time—will be adding a new distance, however small, for you to catch up again . . . and so you can never catch up," the Tortoise concluded.

(A version of Zeno's paradox of motion adapted from Plato's Parmenides)

A milestone represents a critical point in terms of the development or maturity of a project, program, product, practice or policy. Milestones occur in many aspects of ordinary life. For example, graduation from high school or college may represent key milestones for many. Getting married or having a child are other familiar milestones. Having a key birthday (e.g., becoming of age to vote) could be a milestone for some. In these cases, while a milestone is linked to a point in time, in and of itself the milestone has no duration. At one moment one is not 18 and at the next moment one is 18 and becomes eligible to vote and enlist in the military (in the USA, that is).

Milestones are widely embraced by the project management community as tools to keep an effort on its projected timeline and properly coordinated across the tasks and activities associated with the project (Project Management Institute, 2013). Milestones can be created to represent specific events (e.g., a quality review or a field test) or progressive stages in the maturation of an effort. In general, milestones serve as markers of progress. Milestones occur at a designated point in time but take up no time and require no resources in and of themselves. However, evaluations are often put in place after key milestones are passed, and evaluations obviously require time and resources.

Some efforts are divided into phases or stages, often associated with a period time (e.g., year 1, year 2, and so on). In some of those cases when the effort is externally funded, a report on what has been achieved may be required by the funding agency. An upcoming requirement for a status report can trigger a formative evaluation that will be shared with the funding agency. Such an evaluation is focused on reporting specific things that have been accomplished (e.g., training materials developed, training completed with 75 percent of targeted users, etc.). In some cases, a milestone can be linked to what is called a deliverable (a tangible or intangible object that is expected to be delivered to another group or to a customer or to a funding agency). A periodic report or status update is a deliverable often required by funding agencies at key points as an effort matures (e.g., monthly, annually, etc.).

It may be reasonable to link a milestone to a critical aspect of the effort (e.g., a product passes internal review or a technology has just been field tested). In these cases, a formative evaluation is focused on things that might be changed or improved. One might decide to distinguish this kind of evaluation as an *internal evaluation* and the kind tied to a milestone report to a funding agency as an *external evaluation*. It may happen that different evaluation teams are involved in internal and external evaluations, although that is somewhat rare and usually associated with very large efforts that span multiple years.

Whereas a funding agency may set requirements for external evaluations, the team(s) responsible for designing, developing and deploying the effort can and probably should set internal milestones and structure internal formative evaluations around those internal milestones, engaging key persons and representative users early and often (Collins, 2005; Griffith, 2012). The reason for doing that is simply that the primary function of evaluation is to help ensure the success of the effort to the greatest extent possible.

Technology Integration Efforts

The efforts of focus in this volume are related to the effective integration of technology into learning and instruction. Unfortunately, there are too few cases of systemic and sustained success in this area with less than 30 percent of American students actively using technology to support their learning (Moeller & Reitzes, 2011).

Example Milestones for Different Kinds of Efforts

Project Milestones

Consider a project involving the introduction of a flipped classroom approach in an elementary school. Recall that a flipped classroom approach generally involves having students read and review primary presentation materials outside the classroom and doing activities and exercises applying the concepts, principles and other information in meaningful and practical situations in the classroom with guidance and support from the teacher. Potential milestones could include the following:

- gaining the support of school leadership; this could follow a number of presentations and discussions with school leaders and key staff support personnel (e.g., librarians, technology coordinators, special education specialists, etc.); determination of support could be obtained by direct questions and any formal process in place for such matters;

- gaining the support of most teachers; this could follow a number of presentations and discussions with teachers, probably grouped by grade level and subject; problems involved could be elicited along with solution approaches; determination of support could be obtained by a simple end of sequence survey and any formal process in place for such matters;
- identification of strategies for grade levels and subjects; this could follow the previous set of discussions and be accomplished using a form to elicit, compile, circulate and resolve specific strategies and support technologies to be used;
- training of teachers; this could be accomplished in a series of sessions to develop elaborations of the strategies and specific technologies to be used;
- preparation of materials and technologies; this should be accomplished with teachers and support specialists working together;
- implementation of a first-phase tryout with a series of lessons in selected grade levels and subject areas;
- refinement of strategies and technologies; any problems discovered in the tryouts should be addressed and corrected; fidelity of implementation study number 1;
- implementation of a second-phase tryout with the entire courses of those involved in phase one;
- refinements, additional training and any needed support put in place; fidelity of implementation study number 2;
- full-scale implementation initiated; and
- full-scale implementation evaluated; fidelity of implementation study number 3.

An impact study might be accomplished once the project has been in place for a couple of years. An appropriate in-class activity or discussion forum topic might involve a discussion of these milestones and others that might be appropriate.

Program Milestones

Consider the case of introducing a new online master's degree program in sports management at the undergraduate college level. Suppose the college has a successful residential program in place with steady enrollments. The motivation is to reach students who want the degree but are employed part-time or unable to commit to a full-time residential program. The existing program focuses on the last two years of a baccalaureate that focuses on such things as (a) familiarization with college athletic programs, (b) marketing and financial management of programs, (c) coaching and physical education practices, (d) legal issues involving sports programs, (e) leisure and recreational sports activities, and (f) commercial and professional sports activities. Program milestones might include the following:

- data collection and analysis of other online undergraduate sports management programs; sharing findings with the program team marks the completion of the milestone, and can contribute to the establishment of goals for the new program;
- review of the last five years of residential enrollments, retention and graduation data; sharing findings with the program team marks the completion of the milestone, and can contribute to the establishment of goals for the new program;
- determining faculty and college support; following discussion with current faculty and college administrators, a decision to proceed should be reached using any formal processes for such a decision that might be in place;
- identification of a small number of current courses to be re-designed and developed for online delivery;
- design and development of the initial trial courses; a fidelity of implementation study could complete this milestone;
- deployment of the trial courses; a second fidelity of implementation study could be conducted and data on enrollments and problems encountered included in the report of the study;
- development of all of the courses to be offered in the first year of the new online program with tryouts with locally enrolled students; a third fidelity of implementation study could be completed followed by revisions to design and develop guidelines and processes;
- deployment of the first year's courses while the second year's courses are being developed; a fidelity of implementation study of the first year courses should include enrollments, retention, grade and performance analysis, and perceptions of students and teachers; and
- full-scale deployment of the new program; again a fidelity of implementation study should be conducted along with plans to track data pertinent to the goals of the program, with an impact study to follow in several years.

An appropriate in-class activity or discussion forum topic might involve a discussion of these milestones and others that might be appropriate.

Product Milestones

Suppose the institution is considering a change in its learning management system (LMS). In this context, an LMS is a comprehensive software environment that supports the design, development, deployment, assessment and management of face-to-face, hybrid, and fully online courses. The institution is now using one of widely used commercial systems that also happens to be one of the most expensive in terms of institutional costs. That system has been linked to the registrar's enrollment and grade-reporting systems at some expense. The motivation for a change is reduced funds available to the institution due to cutbacks in state and federal support. Because the system has been in place for more than five years, a great deal of resistance is expected. The following are possibly relevant milestones for such an effort:

- review of existing costs and benefits of the current system; a report marks the conclusion of this milestone;
- review of systems used by comparable institutions; a report marks the conclusion of this milestone;
- review of the research literature on LMSs; a report marks the conclusion of this milestone;
- determination of faculty and students' experiences; this could be accomplished by using one of many surveys used at other institutions recently (doing so allows for the potential to compare results with other institutions);
- institutional decision to implement a process to determine whether a new LMS is needed and which one it should be; this should be accomplished by whatever formal procedure is appropriate;
- establishment of an institutional team to review potential systems and organize faculty and student tryouts; the team should include a good mix of faculty, relevant administrators and technical support persons and students; this should be accomplished by whatever formal procedure is appropriate;
- identification of perhaps five potential LMSs, including the current system; the team files a report on how it arrived at the selection of those five;
- presentations and tryouts on campus of the five systems; the teams organize visits from the providers that include opportunities for many faculty, students and technical support persons to try out the new systems over a reasonable number of days;
- survey of faculty, students and technical support persons with regard to the five systems; again, existing instruments might be used to allow for comparison of findings at other institutions; analysis and publication of the results mark the successful completion of this milestone;
- analysis of costs to implement and maintain each system developed and shared with administrators;
- selection of the replacement system; and
- process to implement the new system established; this might be accomplished in a series of stages with selected courses and faculty initially; the process might include plans to convert existing courses to the new systems; the process might also allow for some faculty to continue using the legacy system for one or two years while the new system gains traction and any problems and issues are resolved; the process should include detailed plans for both a formative evaluation (fidelity of implementation study) and a summative evaluation (impact study).

An appropriate in-class activity or discussion forum topic might involve a discussion of these milestones and others that might be appropriate.

Practice Milestones

Suppose that, consistent with new educational standards that emphasize collaboration and interdisciplinarity, an effort to implement small learning groups that cut across middle school grades is being considered. Based on some research reports that suggest that this approach might improve learning, one afternoon per week has been targeted as an initial time for such groups, based on an agreement of teachers and administrators. The following milestones might be appropriate:

- establishment of goals and measureable outcomes for the practice; this can be accomplished based on the prior discussions and perhaps a Delphi process to ensure that all perspectives are represented and heard;
- identification of the day and time slot and how existing coursework will be adjusted to accommodate the new effort;
- identification of the areas into which students can be grouped; groups should be of an easily managed size (e.g., five to 15) and consistent with the ability of teachers, teacher aides and participating parents to support the groups; groups might be allowed to organize their own activities within the context of very general goals established for each group;
- establishment of a practice for grouping and re-grouping students;
- deployment of the multi-grade groups in the second semester of the year as an initial tryout; a formative evaluation could be conducted to mark the completion of this milestone;
- refinement and re-design of groups, goals and activities in compliance with recommendations from the formative evaluation; and
- deployment of the collaboration groups in a first full-year tryout; this milestone could be marked by a fidelity of implementation study that might suggest further refinements to the practice.

An impact study should be conducted after a second or third year of the practice to determine to what extent goals have been met and any effects on test-scores, disciplinary activities or other possibly relevant factors. An appropriate in-class activity or discussion forum topic might involve a discussion of these milestones and others that might be appropriate.

Policy Milestones

A school district is planning to implement a bring-your-own-device (BYOD) policy given the widespread reports of the potential benefits of mobile learning in and outside the classroom. It is known that some parents will object on the basis of lack of technology at home and the potential of student access to inappropriate sites. In addition, federal funding is linked to blocking access to potentially harmful sites (see www.fcc.gov/guides/childrens-internet-protection-act for such a law in the USA). Given the decision to proceed and the potential resistance, the following milestones might be relevant:

- establishment of a timeline for activities, milestones, and evaluations of the policy enactment that includes some or all of the following;
- establishment of a policy enactment team that includes administrators, lead teachers and concerned parents;
- publication of a theory of change document to justify the planned policy change;
- identification of a multi-year, multi-step process that allows for the identification of problems and proposed solutions; this should include the elaboration of relevant fidelity of implementation studies; likely stages include elementary, middle and high school stages, and perhaps further refinements within those stages;
- identification of measureable goals for the new policy, including short-, medium- and long-term goals;
- completion of a cost–benefits analysis of the new effort; this could be based on phasing out print textbooks entirely and having all learning materials provided in a digital format that could be put on each student's device;
- development of a detailed implementation plan that includes the theory of change, a logic model, fidelity of implementation studies and an impact study;
- an analysis of providing each student with a specific WiFi portable device with blocking of harmful sites built-in and some materials pre-installed and others to be made available as they become available; this analysis should probably include the beliefs and reactions of parents since the potential to meet their concerns is important; publication of a report marks the completion of this milestone;
- an analysis of whether and to what extent planned instructional materials exist in digital format and can be installed and used on a portable device; publication of a report marks the completion of this milestone;
- training teachers on the use of mobile devices to support learning and instruction; this is a non-trivial part of the policy that should be conducted over a period of time with refresher and renewal training periodically available; teachers should be provided with the same device to be made available to students (assuming the district will be providing the devices as an alternative to buying print-based textbooks);
- initial tryout with a test group (e.g., all of the third grade classrooms in a particular school that includes student use, teacher perceptions, student perceptions and parent reactions); a formative evaluation report can mark the completion of this milestone; and
- expansion of the test case to an entire school, again with a formative evaluation or fidelity of implementation report marking the completion of the milestone.

An appropriate in-class activity or discussion forum topic might involve a discussion of these milestones and others that might be appropriate.

Test Your Understanding

Which of the following statements are true and why?

1. Milestones should be created for each and every activity involved in an effort.
2. Similar milestones can be developed for different kinds of efforts.
3. One or more formative evaluations or fidelity of implementation studies should be conducted for each effort.
4. For each effort sketched in this chapter, briefly describe a relevant fidelity of implementation study and how it might improve the effort.
5. Once the goals for an effort are identified, it should be possible to identify an impact study for that effort.
6. For each of the efforts sketched above, briefly indicate what might constitute a relevant impact study.

A Representative Educational Technology Challenge

Consider that you have been selected to lead one of the sample efforts briefly sketched in this chapter. Develop a short (two to five double-spaced pages) white paper that provides an executive summary of the effort, including the purpose, scope and likely benefits and barriers. Include an initial theory of change statement supported with relevant research and development literature citations, and a logic model that includes inputs, outputs and at least short- and medium-term outcomes. Identify relevant assumptions that have been made and indicate relevant expectations with regard to implementation and support.

Learning Activities

For one of the example situations presented in this chapter, develop initial goals, a theory of change and a logic model with elaborated input and output columns; then develop a comprehensive list of relevant milestones for key activities, and indicate which ones should trigger an evaluation and why.

Links

Basecamp app—see https://basecamp.com/

Educational technology and mobile learning: ten web tools to help integrate technology—see www.educatorstechnology.com/2013/02/10-web-tools-to-help-you-integrate.html

FCC Children's Internet Protection Act—see www.fcc.gov/guides/childrens-internet-protection-act

Other Resources

ITtoolkit: Using milestones to track project progress and accomplishments—see www.ittoolkit.com/how-to-it/projects/project-milestones.html

MindTools: Project management—see www.mindtools.com/pages/main/newMN_PPM.htm

Smartsheet blog by Kelly Anthony: When to Use Milestones in Your Project Plan—see www.smartsheet.com/blog/support-tip-milestones-in-project-management

BeorgiaStandards.org: Teacher tools for integrating technology—see www.georgiastandards.org/Resources/Pages/Tools/toolsandlinks.aspx

Usabililty.gov website for project management basics—see www.usability.gov/what-and-why/project-management.html

Webdesigner: 30 greatest online project management and collaboration tools for easy communication—see www.1stwebdesigner.com/project-management-collaboration-tools/

References

Collins, J. (2005). *Good to great and the social sectors: A monography to accompany Good to Great.* New York: Harper.

Griffith, T. L. (2012). *The plugged-in manager: Get in tune with your people, technology, and organization to thrive.* San Francisco, CA: Jossey-Bass.

Moeller, B., & Reitzes, T. (2011). *Integrating technology with student-centered learning* [Report to the Nellie Mae Education Foundation]. Quincy, MA: Nellie Mae Foundation. Retrieved from www.nmefoundation.org/getmedia/befa9751-d8ad-47e9–949d-bd649f7c0044/integrating

Project Management Institute (2013). *A guide to the project management body of knowledge* (5th ed.). Newtown Square, PA: Project Management Institute.

seventeen
Ongoing Formative Evaluations

> *Mathematicians are like managers—they want improvement without change.*
>
> *(Edsger Dijkstra)*

The general purpose of a formative evaluation is to improve that which is being evaluated. Because many efforts involving educational technology take years to mature and be fully implemented, there is a need to take seriously the notion of multiple formative evaluations or multiple fidelity of implementation studies. Of course not all formative evaluations involve a detailed fidelity of implementation study as those are relevant when there has been a design specification followed by a development effort and possibly a trial deployment or test with representative users. Other kinds of formative evaluations are appropriate depending on the status of the effort and its maturity. In all cases, however, a formative evaluation should have a specific purpose, and that purpose should at least indirectly be aimed at improving the effort.

The use of educational technology for formative evaluation has long been established (Huber & Gay, 1984). In this chapter, the focus is on the formative evaluation of educational technologies, which is less well explored. If one considers an effort from a life-cycle perspective, then one might identify the phases in Table 17.1 where a formative evaluation of some kind is appropriate.

Test Your Understanding

Answer the following questions as indicated:

1. Often only one formative evaluation is needed for an effort.
   ____ True ____ False
2. A document review can be part of a formative evaluation.
   ____ True ____ False

TABLE 17.1 Formative evaluations throughout a life cycle

Life Cycle Phase	Appropriate Formative Evaluations
Needs Assessment	Review of expressed needs and the relationship of needs, goals and a mission or vision statement, focusing on who was involved and why; surveys, interviews and focus groups are often used
Requirements Analysis	Review of proposed solutions and the associated technologies and support required, focusing on those involved and the alignment of proposed solutions with goals and needs; interviews are critical
Design	Review of design specifications with a focus on goals and the perceptions of key persons involved in the effort; using specific criteria to guide the evaluation of the design is desirable
Development	Fidelity of implementation study focused on adherence to goals and the design specifications
Field Test	Fidelity of implementation study focused on usability, user reactions and perceptions, and refinement of the technology
Refinement and Deployment	Fidelity of implementation study focused on use, ongoing issues and potential impact on learning and instruction; this fidelity of implementation study should be as comprehensive as possible as it will provide a basis for explaining the results of an impact study
Management	Review of how well the effort continues to attain goals and meet objects; a focus on goals, costs, support and user perceptions; document reviews are often involved in such an evaluation

3. Surveying the perceptions of representative users is typically appropriate for impact studies and not formative evaluations.

_____ True _____ False

4. A fidelity of implementation study can be used to improve the quality of an effort.

_____ True _____ False

Formative Evaluation and Formative Assessment

The relationship of formative assessments of students and formative evaluations of educational technology efforts was discussed in Chapter 1 and elsewhere in this volume. It is worth revisiting that relationship in the context of a discussion about the importance of ongoing formative evaluations. Few would question the value of proving ongoing formative assessments and feedbacks to students during a course or throughout a program. The general goal of those formative assessments is primarily to help learners make progress in terms of understanding and performance. In addition, those formative assessments can be used to inform evaluators about what is working well with which learners in the context of evaluating an educational technology effort.

Formative evaluations are also important to perform multiple times and often on an ongoing basis (e.g., with regard to practices, policies and programs). There is generally the possibility for improvement, and formative evaluations are aimed at improving those efforts.

It may happen that an educational technology effort is aimed specifically at improving learning performance and understanding. In such a case, formative assessments are a natural and vital part of a formative evaluation. Knowing which learners are helped [or hindered] in what ways with different learning tasks can help the evaluation team suggest refinements to an ongoing effort.

In any case, the primary purpose of formative evaluations in the broad domain of educational technology is to improve a project, program, product, practice or policy that involves educational technology. That purpose is directly aligned with the evaluator's primary responsibility—namely, to help the effort succeed.

A Representative Educational Technology Challenge

As an effort is scaled up to a larger group of users and perhaps multiple organizations, it becomes increasingly important to conduct ongoing formative evaluations and make iterative refinements. Doing so will ensure that the effort is likely to succeed; in addition, ongoing formative evaluations have a tendency to improve participation and perceptions (see Weston, 2004). In some cases, a fidelity of implementation study can be used to predict failure as well as explain the degree to which an effort has succeeded (Crawford, Carpenter II, Wilson, Schmeister, & McDonald, 2012; Durand, Decker, & Kirkman, 2014). A particular challenging situation occurs when a fidelity of implementation study indicates that an effort has drifted off course, and the evaluator or evaluation team is put in the position of recommending an action such as finding a different software provider or changing the leadership of the effort in order to avoid likely failure of the effort to attain intended outcomes. Find an occurrence of such a situation in the literature and describe what was done; as an alternative, describe a realistic situation involving an evaluation report that indicates that the effort is off course and indicate what you might do and why.

Learning Activities

Select one of the two CRESST reports listed in the LINKS section below. Determine the kinds of evaluation involved (formative or summative), and provide a two page executive summary synthesizing the results of the evaluation report.

Links

The implementation and effects of the mathematics design collaborative (MDC): Early findings from Kentucky ninth-grade algebra 1 courses—see www.cse.ucla.edu/products/reports.php?action=fetch&id=846

The implementation and effects of the literacy design collaborative (LDC): Early findings in sixth-grade advanced reading courses—see www.cse.ucla.edu/products/reports.php?action=fetch&id=846

Resources

National Center for Research on Evaluation, Standards, & Student Testing (CRESST)—see www.cse.ucla.edu/products/articles.php

References

Crawford, L., Carpenter II, D. M., Wilson, M. T., Schmeister, M., & McDonald, M. (2012). Testing the relation between fidelity of implementation and student outcomes in math. *Assessment for Effective Intervention, 37*(4), 224–235.

Durand, R., Decker, P. J., & Kirkman, D. M. (2014). Evaluation methodologies for estimating the likelihood of program implementation failure. *American Journal of Evaluation, 35*(3), 404–418.

Huber, V. L., & Gay, G. (1984). Use of educational technology for formative evaluation. *New Directions for Adult and Continuing Education, 24*(1), 55–64.

Weston, T. (2004). Formative evaluation for implementation: Evaluating educational technology applications and lessons. *American Journal of Evaluation, 25*(1), 51–64.

eighteen
Dynamic Improvements to Ensure Success

There's no good idea that can't be improved on.
(Michael Eisner)

One of the things that makes it difficult to conduct educational research and evaluation is the dynamic nature of learning and instruction. The term 'dynamic' implies change over time. What kinds of things change in an educational context?

First, it is necessary to identify the kinds of things that comprise an educational context. What are the building blocks of a learning environment or an instructional system? One might think of that question as analogous to the question in physics with regard to the building blocks of all physical things. Early Greek scientists (e.g., Empedocles) identified four elements that comprise all things: (a) earth, (b) air, (c) fire and (d) water (see www.plato.stanford.edu/entries/empedocles/). Aristotle takes up the question of the basic building blocks of all things as only a starting point for accounting for what is seen and experienced, since issues involving time, change and motion are important (see www.classics.mit.edu/Aristotle/physics.1.i.html). Questions about change over time and motion turn out to be much more difficult than questions from a static point of view about what exists.

The point here is to suggest a basic point of departure with regard to the building blocks of educational systems, and then consider time, change and movement. What comes to mind first as the basic components of an educational system include (a) students, (b) teachers, (c) things to be learned and (d) resources. This is analogous to an earth–air–fire–water perspective. While these things obviously exist, there are further refinements to take into account.

Students have many different characteristics that influence their interests and activities and for which instructional strategies and resources are likely to be effective. If one accepts that statement, then it follows that there exist dynamic relationships among the basic educational components.

Educational System Dynamics

Moreover, neither the basic components nor the elaborated levels within each component are static. Students are not uniform. In addition, a particular student is likely to change and evolve over time. The same reasoning applies to teachers. Curricula are not static, so the things to be learned also change, as do the resources that can support learning and instruction. It seems that nearly everything in an educational system can change. Even the seating arrangement in a classroom can change, as can the interface of an online learning environment. As Spector (2015a) has argued, a systems perspective leads one naturally to consider the dynamics of a system. An educational system is particularly dynamic due to the fact that humans are involved—students, teachers, support personnel and so on. People are not nearly as predictable as a machine. As a result, when designing, developing and deploying a people-intensive system, it is especially important to see how a wide variety of humans interact with and are affected by that system.

This line of reasoning applies in a general way to educational technology efforts. While the technology itself may be more or less static (e.g., a tablet device, an interactive smartboard, etc.), the use of a technology is very likely to be dynamic and vary with those involved, the context, the purpose and more. Since the use of a technology is highly variable and dependent to a great extent on the people involved, conducting research and evaluation is much more challenging than other forms of research and evaluation.

An educational technology researcher would be well advised not to focus on a particular technology (e.g., Blackboard, Facebook, Prezi, etc.) but, rather, to focus on the characteristics and affordances of a technology that might support and enhance learning. Particular technologies come and go, but the innovations and affordances of those technologies are likely to be available in newer technologies.

Educational technology evaluators, on the other hand, are often required to focus on specific technologies involved in a particular effort. This is one thing that distinguishes evaluation and research in the field of educational technology. Still, forward thinking educational technology evaluators will realize that the next iteration of the effort, or a subsequent effort, may well involve a new technology. As a result, finding relationships at the level of specific capabilities and affordances and outcomes is highly desirable in educational technology evaluation efforts.

Characteristics of complex, dynamic systems include (a) many interrelated components; (b) non-linear relationships among various components; (c) delayed effects when changes are introduced; and (d) shifting structural effects as different components become differently emphasized and influential (Dörner, 1996; Sterman, 1994). All of these characteristics can be found in educational systems (Riasat, Rixvi, Zehara, & Arain, 2008; Spector, 2015b)). For example, one might think of the students in a classroom as a collection of interrelated and interacting agents that influence the behavior of the learning environment over time. The relationship between a student and a teacher is often non-linear, for example when a teacher's patience is exhausted or a student is offended or surprised by a teacher's remarks. When implementing a particular technology, advocates of that technology are often inclined to expect immediate results in spite of a great deal of evidence that suggests that initially performance may take a dip followed by a slow gain over time in terms of desired outcomes. When introducing augmented reality or an interactive simulation into a learning situation, the influence of the teacher may shift from that of source of information to that of coach or guide or mentor.

Educational systems are inherently complex and dynamic. The use of educational technologies is also complex and dynamic. Often, technologies are not used as planned, and use is likely to change over time as habits and expectations replace prescribed forms of use. As a result of the dynamic nature of educational systems and educational technologies, ongoing evaluations are required in order to keep up with changes in use, requirements, goals, resources, support and so on.

Test Your Understanding

Indicate your response to each of the following tasks:

1. List at least six components of a representative learning environment or instructional system.
2. Indicate three ways in which there are dynamics (change over time) in a representative learning environment or instructional system.
3. Describe at least one non-linear relationship among the components of a representative learning environment or instructional system.
4. Describe a case of delayed effects with regard to the introduction of an educational technology into a learning environment or instructional system.

A Representative Educational Technology Challenge

Imagine a progressive high school has decided that the last year of high school should be completely focused on developing twenty-first century skills in students, some of whom will be pursuing technical and vocational careers and some of whom will be pursuing academic studies in a university context. This final year is intended not only to build twenty-first century skills but also to build an understanding of the world that cuts across multiple disciplines and perspectives. Imagine further that you are the leader of a team that is charged with developing a plan for such a program within the next two years. How might you organize such an effort? What kinds of formative evaluations would you include in the plan to maximize the likelihood of developing an effective plan?

Learning Activities

Consider the link to twenty-first century learning environments in the LINKS section below. Provide a two-page synthesis of that document that includes a definition of a twenty-first century learning environment and any policies and practices that are mentioned in the report. Provide a one-page appendix that sketches a framework for both formative and summative evaluation of a twenty-first century learning environment.

Links

21st Century Learning Environments (Partnership for 21st Century Skills)—see www.p21.org/storage/documents/le_white_paper-1.pdf

Resources

Handbook for Research on Educational Communications and Technologies (4th ed.)—see www.aect.site-ym.com/?page=handbook_of_research (for access through AECT) or www.springer.com/us/book/9781461431848

References

Dörner, D. (1996). *The logic of failure: Why things go wrong and what we can do to make them right*, trans. R. & R. Kimber. New York: Henry Holt & Co.

Riasat, A., Rizvi, S. S., Zehara, F., & Arain, F. (2008). The role of system dynamics in learning environments. In M. Iskander (Ed.), *Innovative techniques in instruction technology, e-learning, and education* (pp. 538–541). New York: Springer.

Spector, J. M. (2015a). *Foundations of educational technology: Integrative approaches and interdisciplinary perspectives* (2nd ed.). New York: Routledge.

Spector, J. M. (2015b). System dynamics. In J. M. Spector (Ed.), *The SAGE encyclopedia of educational technology* (pp. 693–697). Thousand Oaks, CA: Sage Publications.

Sterman, J. D. (1994). Learning in and about complex systems. *System Dynamics Review, 10*(2–3), 291–330.

nineteen
Collecting and Analyzing Data

Data! Data! Data! I can't make bricks without clay.
(Sherlock Holmes, from Arthur Conan Doyle's
The Adventure of Copper Breeches*)*

Evaluation and research studies should be based on evidence that has been collected according to established protocols and analyzed according to recognized methods. There are basically two types of data that are collected and analyzed: qualitative and quantitative. Qualitative data come in the form of focus group discussions, interviews, observations, and answers to open-ended questions on surveys; basically, data collected from individuals or groups that require interpretation are common forms of qualitative data. Quantitative data typically come in the form of numbers and are generally divided into *categorical data*, such as counts of responses in each category in a Likert scale survey instrument, or *continuous data*, such as test scores, age, income and other such items that have continuous values along a logically progressive scale.

Each has advantages and limitations along with appropriate methods to analyze findings. Qualitative data can provide insight and add understanding in the course of an evaluation; they are especially useful in explaining the results of an impact study that might be primarily quantitative in nature. On the other hand, quantitative data are readily analyzed and generally produce concrete results. However, quantitative data may not provide an adequate basis for explaining outcomes, especially in an impact study; moreover, advanced data analysis techniques require special expertise (e.g., designing and analyzing a study involving hierarchical linear modeling; see www.pareonline.net/getvn.asp?v=7&n=1). Analyzing qualitative data can turn out to be time-consuming and labor-intensive, as coding is required as is a determination of the reliability of the coding; moreover there is a concern about interpretation bias and subjectivity with regard to qualitative data.

One outcome of the advantages and disadvantages of each type of data is an increasing emphasis on mixed-method evaluation and research studies that involve both qualitative and quantitative data and methods (Crewsell & Clark, 2011; Johnson & Onwuegbuzie, 2004; Schifferdecker & Reed, 2009). In the context of an evaluation study that includes both formative and summative studies, mixed methods are essential, especially with regard to fidelity of implementation studies and in explaining the results of an impact study.

An evaluator (or a researcher) needs to plan in advance the data required to perform the analysis needed. There is a trade-off decision between collecting too much data and too little. One can easily be overwhelmed by the amount of data collected. However, overlooking critical data is difficult to overcome after the fact. The general guideline is to plan data collection and analysis early so as to be sure that necessary data are collected and not overlooked. When in doubt with regard to the need to collect specific data (e.g., whether or not certain demographic data are needed), it is generally advisable to collect those data, especially if there is minimal impact on participation and/or human subjects approval. Evaluators, such as researchers, need to take into account the impact on the rights of individuals and comply with any and all human subjects approval processes that may be involved. Institutional review does apply to evaluation studies, especially those that are intended for publication.

Qualitative Data Collection and Analysis

An evaluator (or a researcher) needs to identify the types of qualitative data required for the study and develop a plan to review and organize the data prior to analysis. With much qualitative data it is then important to code and/or categorize those data prior to a process for interpreting the findings. For example, suppose a formative evaluation study involves what is being said in discussion forums in an online course. The purpose to determine how discussions might shift over time and across topics. A coding scheme could be developed based on what is being said, as in a grounded theory approach (developing codes extracted from the data), or an a priori coding scheme (using predetermined codes) might be used. Each approach has advantages and limitations; the point here is to consider which approach might be applicable prior to conducting the evaluation study.

Commonly used qualitative data analysis tools include Atlas.ti (www.atlasti.com/qualitative-data-analysis-software/), MAXQDA (see www.maxqda.com/qualitative-data-analysis-software) and NVivo (www.qsrinternational.com/products_nvivo.aspx). Other tools are available and more are likely to become available. Using a tool that has been used in similar studies may have the advantage of allowing for a comparison of findings, which can add credibility to the findings of the current evaluation study.

Quantitative Data Collection and Analysis

As with all data collection efforts, the data to be collected and analyzed should be identified as early as possible in the effort—typically in the planning stage. In summative evaluation/impact studies, the data to be collected and analyzed is often directly linked to the problem situation and goals. For example, the perceived problem might be low test scores and a low graduation rate, in which case the outcomes to be studied in the impact study are test scores or graduation rates, both of which are quantitative. Quantitative data are often directly linked to the problem situation and goals, so they naturally become the focus of an impact study. However, quantitative data are frequently involved in fidelity of implementation studies that involve user perceptions and reactions that can be collected using survey instruments with categorical scales. As stated many times in this book, formative evaluation/fidelity of implementation studies often involve mixed methods, including both qualitative and quantitative data in the analysis.

It is beyond the scope of this chapter or volume to cover data collection and analysis methods in detail. However, a few guidelines are appropriate. In the planning phase, it should be determined which data will be collected and how it will be analyzed. Sources of data should be as reliable as possible. For example, in determining graduation rates, the official rates reported by a school to the state would be preferred over an answer to the question on a questionnaire by a school administrator. Those analyzing the data should be well trained and experienced, as that adds to the confidence that can be placed in findings. For example, a first-year graduate student is not likely to be as well trained as a seasoned professional; it might be wise to pair a graduate student with an experienced mentor to ensure that the analysis is properly executed.

With quantitative data, there is occasionally a need to delete incomplete data records or discard extremely different responses that might reflect an unwanted prejudice. When this is done, it should be documented and explained in the evaluation report. Such things comprise what is called a data management system by some funding agencies. Details of how data will be collected, recorded, safeguarded, cleaned or filtered, and analyzed are components of such a data management plan.

As with qualitative data, there are many tools available for analyzing quantitative data. Commonly used quantitative data analysis tools include: Minitab (see www.minitab.com/en-us/), R (The R Project for Statistical Computing; see www.r-project.org/) and SPSS (Statistical Package for Social Sciences; see www-01.ibm.com/software/analytics/spss/). Others are available and more will surely become available. In addition, one can use a spreadsheet program or a system dynamics modeling tool to perform many of the functions required.

Test Your Understanding

Indicate which of the following statements are true:

1. A fidelity of implementation study is usually a quantitative study involving the analysis of responses to a Likert style survey questionnaire.
2. Demographic data (age, years of schooling, family income, etc.) gathered in an evaluation study are examples of qualitative data.
3. One advantage of quantitative data involves the concrete and specific nature of findings.
4. One advantage of qualitative data involves the concrete and specific nature of findings.
5. Qualitative data are not subject to interpretation bias.
6. Quantitative data are not subject to interpretation bias.
7. Instruments to gather qualitative and quantitative data do not in and of themselves require analysis or validation.

A Representative Educational Technology Challenge

Suppose you are asked to evaluate a teacher preparation program with regard to how well it prepares teachers for classroom practice. What might you propose in response to the following questions:

- Which teacher preparation programs might be used for comparison or as a baseline?
- How long should the study be, including years in the teacher preparation followed by years in a classroom environment?
- Which quantitative data might be gathered and analyzed in the teaching preparation program and subsequently in the classroom environment?
- Which qualitative data might be gathered and analyzed in the teaching preparation program and subsequently in the classroom environment?
- How relevant might be the perceptions and attitudes of trainee teachers, university instructors, school administrators and teaching colleagues, and how might such perceptions be gathered and analyzed?
- What instruments might be used to gather relevant data?

Learning Activities

Examine the evaluation plan in Appendix A. Identify each type of qualitative and quantitative data involved in that plan. Explain how that evaluation plan, parts of the evaluation plan, could be conceptualized as a mixed methods study.

Links

Analyzing Qualitative Data for Evaluation (CDC, 2009)—see www.cdc.gov/healthyyouth/evaluation/pdf/brief19.pdf

Analyzing Quantitative Data for Evaluation (CDC, 2009)—see www.cdc.gov/healthyyouth/evaluation/pdf/brief20.pdf

Mixed Methods: Practical Possibilities for Evaluation (Greene, 1995)—see www.hfrp.org/evaluation/the-evaluation-exchange/issue-archive/evaluating-school-linked-services/mixed-methods-practical-possibilities-for-evaluation

Resources

Centers for Disease Control and Prevention, Data Collection & Analysis—see www.cdc.gov/healthyyouth/evaluation/data.htm

Introduction to Mixed Methods in Impact Evaluation by Michael Bamberger (2012)—see www.interaction.org/sites/default/files/Mixed%20Methods%20in%20Impact%20Evaluation%20(English).pdf

Mixed Methods in Educational Research, Research Council of Norway—see www.uv.uio.no/ils/personer/vit/kirstik/publikasjoner-pdf-filer/klette.-mixed-methods.pdf

Pell Institute Evaluation Toolkit: Quantitative Data—see www.toolkit.pellinstitute.org/evaluation-guide/analyze/analyze-quantitative-data/

Pell Institute Evaluation Toolkit: Qualitative Data—see www.toolkit.pellinstitute.org/evaluation-guide/analyze/analyze-qualitative-data/

References

Crewsell, J. W., & Clark, V. L. P. (2011). *Designing and conducting mixed methods research* (2nd ed.). Thousand Oaks, CA: Sage Publications.

Johnson, R. B., & Onwuegbuzie, A. J. (2004). Mixed methods research: A research paradigm whose time has come. *Educational Researcher, 33*(7), 14–26.

Schifferdecker, K. E., & Reed, V. A. (2009). Using mixed methods research in medical education: Basic guidelines for researchers. *Medical Education, 43*(7), 637–644.

twenty
Informing and Improving Policy Implementation

No . . . policy . . . has any chance of success if it is born in the minds of a few and carried in the hearts of none.
(attributed to Henry Kissinger,
President Nixon's Secretary of State)

In the course of reviewing the literature on evaluating educational technology, there was very little found that addressed evaluating policies and practices (Harris & Walling, 2014; Kozma & Vota, 2014). A policy is a formal statement that is intended to mandate specific activities and practices with regard to various situations for a variety of purposes; policies are aimed at specific goals and often developed in support of a mission or vision statement. There are a number of policies and policy briefs that one can find that could be the subject of evaluations. However, such evaluations are quite rare. One notable exception is a retrospective on American educational policies in the years 1983—2003 (Culp, Honey, & Mandinach, 2003). That report addressed three questions: (a) What motivated investments in educational technologies? (b) What steps were taken to ensure effective implementation? and (c) What assumptions were made and how have they changed?

The reasons for investing in educational technologies included the potential to (a) support teaching and learning; (b) to serve as a positive change agent; and (c) to improve economic competitiveness. Research in these three areas is not at all conclusive with regard to technology having realized the indicated potential.

Implementation concerns included seven recommendations: (1) improve infrastructure and access; (2) create more high quality content and software; (3) provide ongoing professional development for teachers; (4) increase funding; (5) clarify specific roles for involved stakeholders; (6) increase and diversify research and evaluation; and (7) periodically review and update policies and practices. These recommendations are indeed critical for effective implementation of educational technology policies. In some cases, progress has been made. For example, obviously the infrastructure and access in the USA and elsewhere has improved dramatically since 2003; however, there are places in America and around the world where infrastructure and access is clearly inadequate or deficient. Probably some progress has been made in other areas. However, the recommendation for sustained high-quality professional development for teachers remains largely unfulfilled, in part due to limited funding in general for education. Moreover, teacher preparation programs have not kept pace with the potential for effective integration of educational technologies (Herring & Smaldino, 2015).

The underlying assumptions motivating investments in educational technology are reasonably well aligned with three broad reasons and potential cited earlier. The conclusion of the 2003 report are twofold: (a) the needs and challenges for investing in educational technologies change due to new technologies, funding limitations and social factors; and (b) there is an inadequate understanding of the systemic nature of educational change and technology integration.

The 2003 retrospective report clearly influenced the 2010 National Education Plan (USDOE, 2010). Similar assumptions and motivations appear in the 2010 Plan. Infrastructure and access are still prioritized, as are many of the seven implementation factors cited in 2003. The emphasis on teacher preparation and professional development appears early in the 2010 report and remains a primary area of emphasis. Given what was identified in the 2003 report, and given that the same kinds of concerns again appear in 2010, one can ask what impact policies are having on practice and improving teaching and learning in the USA.

A survey of schools in Europe in 2013 reported similar persistent concerns (see https://ec.europa.eu/digital-agenda/sites/digital-agenda/files/KK-31-13-401-EN-N.pdf). Specifically, infrastructure was still insufficient and teacher use of technologies to support learning was still quite limited. In Europe, the 2013 ICT (Information and Communications Technology) for Development Forum (see www.adb.org/sites/default/files/publication/161445/ict-forum-2013-education.pdf) indicated significant advantages for ICT in improving teaching and learning in Asia, but it also cited significant limitations and deficiencies, including quality concerns pertaining to distance education, the attitudes and perceptions of teachers and others, insufficient resources, and more. Luschei (2014) cited similar issues involving the implementation of educational technologies in developing countries.

To briefly summarize, it seems that similar policies involving educational technology have arisen around the globe and are generally positive in proposing that technology can significantly improve learning, instruction and eventually economic competitiveness. Similar things have appeared in these policies in the last 20 years—namely, support funding to improve access and infrastructure, provide teacher training and professional development support for the effective integration of technology in learning and instruction, and continue to emphasize innovative technologies and their use to improve and ultimately transform learning and instruction. Given the very strong advocacy of new and emerging technologies and approaches to learning by researchers and scholars, it is not surprising to find such policies (see, for example, the resources below for recent *Horizon Reports* by the New Media Consortium and *the Roadmap for Education Technology* published in 2010).

Apart from the 2003 Retrospective Report, however, these policies have not been evaluated or subjected to critical scrutiny. One might conclude that these policies reflect what policymakers believe that people, or a select group of people (i.e., educators and educational technologies), want to hear. The will and wherewithal to follow through with implementation and effective practice is not apparent when what is happening in education and schools is examined. While there is an accountability culture growing at the lower levels of the education system (i.e., with regard to specific teachers and schools), there is no accountability culture or system at the higher policymaking levels other than election of different decision makers. What can be done? Answering this question is not simple or straightforward, in part because educational systems are inherently complex and linked to other social, economic and political systems. In the next two sections, a few tentative first steps will be suggested.

Linking Policies to Practice

As previously indicated, policies are intentional and formal statements intended to guide practice in order to realize specific goals. A policy without any implications for practice is vacuous. From an evaluation perspective, a policy needs to have two characteristics: (a) one or more goals (needed for an impact study or summative evaluation), and (b) specific implications for practice or implementation steps (needed for a fidelity of implementation study or formative evaluation). In most cases, educational technology policies have associated goals and objectives. However, in many cases, the steps required to successfully implement a policy are not made clear or specific. The result of such a deficiency is that a formative evaluation cannot be accomplished. Without the information and data gathered and analyzed in a formative evaluation, it is difficult to explain any impact that may have been noted or link any changes to specific actions taken in accordance with the policy.

The first requirement for an educational technology policy to be evaluated is that it have the two characteristics indicated above—goals and implementation steps. If either is lacking, the policy should be considered deficient and a request for a revised policy that has both characteristics should be made. Professional evaluators, educators and the general public should insist on having policies that can be evaluated. Rather than being told what one wants to hear, one should have a desire to know why and what is going to be done to improve a situation, as well as when and how those actions are going to be implemented. A common coaching statement in sports is that *follow through is everything.* The goal might be to throw with more accuracy; the implementation is to complete the throw—to follow through. This notion applies to educational technology policies. The goals are often clear and perhaps even measureable. What is all too often lacking is the follow through. The specific actions and steps required for successful attainment of those goals. Follow through in the form of implementation steps is required, and it is one of the evaluator's responsibilities to insist on those steps in order to evaluate a policy.

In terms of the things being evaluated in this book, it should now be clear that evaluating a policy requires the evaluation of the practices associated with implementation of that policy. While some practices are not associated with a policy and can be evaluated independently of a policy, it is not possible to evaluate a policy without the practices and follow-through actions needed to implement the policy.

Evaluating Policies and Practices

It should be clear that evaluating an educational technology policy requires an evaluation of the associated practices and activities associated with the implementation of that policy. While the summative evaluation of an educational technology policy will focus on the original goals of the policy, a summative evaluation of a policy is somewhat rare since policies tend to persist for long periods of time. However, there could and should be periodic summative evaluations of a policy just as one might have periodic summative evaluations of an ongoing program. In the cases of these periodic reviews, however, the primary questions being asked are (a) should the policy be continued—clearly summative, and (b) what aspects of the policy should be changed to improve outcomes— clearly formative. As a consequence, the remaining comments in this section apply to formative evaluations of policies and their associated practices.

An excellent model for the formative evaluation of policies and associated practices is the *2003 Retrospective Report.* The report identified the critical implementation steps of the educational technology policy, and then examined each of those implementation steps with regard to how well it adhered to the plan, how well it was implemented and then supported, and what influence it had on targeted outcomes. The evaluation included a review of many key documents and policy statements, a review of the relevant research and policy studies, and data pertinent to the implementation gathered from a number of sources and reports (e.g., public funding, computer–student ratios, use of computers in schools, etc.).

The *2003 Retrospective Report* relied primarily on the review and analysis of policy statements and related reports. While the findings are reasonably well substantiated, an even stronger evaluation study might include independently gathered information through surveys and interviews of representative stakeholders (policymakers, administrators, teachers, students and parents). As an example, one finding suggests that there is and has been inadequate funding support for the effective implementation of educational technologies, with the result that teacher training and professional development and ongoing maintenance and support are often inadequate. To understand why funding has not kept pace with requirements for successful implementation, it is necessary to go beyond the surface level indicators, such as level or declining funding while needs are increasing due to more students and out-of-date or inadequate infrastructure. Why has funding not been adequate? What else is being funded? Has public support for education declined? Have other things been given a higher priority? What do parents think and believe? What do voters think and believe? Without a deeper analysis of all of those involved in supporting an educational technology policy, it is not possible to find underlying problems and causes for known deficiencies, which makes it impossible to recommend improvements or changes in policy implementation.

A second small step in improving the situation with regard to evaluating policies and practices is conduct a deeper analysis of the actions, decisions and steps taken to implement a policy. A deeper analysis of the practice (actions, decisions and steps) might involve (a) an analysis of the implementation plan in terms of alignment with the goals and purpose of the policy, (b) a quality analysis of each implementation step in terms of how well that step followed the plan for that step and was aligned with overall goals, (c) an analysis of perceptions of all involved with the efficacy of each implementation step, and (d) indications of the extent to which a particular step was influencing targeted interim and final outcomes. Such an analysis could form a robust review and provide a basis for revisions or changes to the policy and subsequent implementation steps.

In conclusion, it is not what one says about the potential impact of a technology or a policy associated with that technology that is critical. What is critical in terms of improving learning, performance and instruction is what is actually done with the technology. It is not about the technology. It is about the use of the technology. Therefore, what is important in evaluating policies and practices is determining what is being done, how well it is being done, and how those activities and uses of a technology might be improved and better supported in order to realize the full potential of the technology.

Test Your Understanding

1. According to the *2003 Retrospective Report*, what reasons motivated investments in educational technology?
2. According to the *2003 Retrospective Report*, name five of the seven implementation steps that were recommended, and then provide evidence that suggests successful implementation (or lack thereof) of one of those implementation steps.
3. Find an educational technology policy at any level that has been evaluated and provide a citation/link and synthesis of that evaluation report.
4. Find an educational technology practice at any level that has been evaluated and provide a citation/link and synthesis of that evaluation report.
5. Describe what is needed in order to plan and conduct formative and summative evaluations of an educational technology policy.

A Representative Educational Technology Challenge

Suppose there is a remote, rural school in a developing country with one multi-grade school that serves three mountain villages. There are no computers in this school. Each classroom has about 50 students, with half at one grade level and the other half at a different grade level. There are three classrooms for first and second graders, third and fourth graders, and fifth and sixth graders. Each classroom has a blackboard, chalk and desks that seat three children; each desk is equipped with one note pad, one writing instrument and one ruler. Currently nearly all students progress according to national standards and pass the mandated test for successful completion of elementary education. To continue on to a secondary school, students have their villages and travel several hours to a city where they live while in school there. Only about 10 percent of the students go on to the secondary level. Of that 10 percent who continue, nearly all complete high school and find jobs in the city, not returning to their villages. The parents have decided that they want to increase the percentage of their children continuing their education from 10 percent to 75 percent. The parents have asked for your advice and assistance. What would you recommend in terms of a policy to guide them?

Learning Activities

Find an educational policy at your institution or state that has been formalized in the last five years. Identify the specific goals of the policy. Indicate what activities and practices are recommended and/or required to carry out the policy. Specify the components of a formative evaluation of the policy.

Links

Policy analysis for California education (Charles Taylor Kerchner, 2013)—see www.edpolicyinca.org/publications/education-technology-policy-21st-century-learning-system.

A retrospective on twenty years of education technology policy—see www2.ed.gov/rschstat/eval/tech/20years.pdf

The 2010 National Education Technology Plan—see www.ed.gov/sites/default/files/netp2010.pdf

Survey of schools: ICT in education (report to the European Commission in 2013)—https://ec.europa.eu/digital-agenda/sites/digital-agenda/files/KK-31–13-401-EN-N.pdf

The 2013 ICT for Development Forum—see www.adb.org/sites/default/files/publication/161445/ict-forum-2013-education.pdf

Resources

A roadmap for education technology (Woolf, 2010; report to NSF)—see www.cra.org/ccc/files/docs/groe/GROE%20Roadmap%20for%20Education%20Technology%20Final%20Report.pdf

The New Media Consortium Horizon Reports—see www.nmc.org

TelEurope—a Website devoted to technology-enhanced learning—see www.teleurope.eu/pg/frontpage

References

Culp, K. M., Honey, M., & Mandinach, E. (2003). *A retrospective on twenty years of educational technology policy*. Washington, DC: Office of Educational Technology. Retrieved from www2.ed.gov/rschstat/eval/tech/20years.pdf

Harris, P., & Walling, D. R. (2014). Policies governing educational technology practice and research. In J. M. Spector, M. D. Merrill, J. Elen, & M. J. Bishop (Eds.), *Handbook of research on educational communications and technology* (4th ed.; pp. 627–640). New York: Springer.

Herring, M. C., & Smaldino, S. E. (2015). TPACK (Technological Pedagogical Content Knowledge): Implications for 21st century education. In J. M. Spector (Ed.), *The SAGE encyclopedia of educational technology* (pp. 785–787). Thousand Oaks, CA: Sage.

Kozma, R. B., & Vota, W. S. (2014). ICT in developing countries: Policies, implementation and impact. In J. M. Spector, M. D. Merrill, J. Elen, & M. J. Bishop (Eds.), *Handbook of research on educational communications and technology* (4th ed.; pp. 885–894). New York: Springer.

Luschei, T. F. (2014). Assessing the costs and benefits of educational technology. In J. M. Spector, M. D. Merrill, J. Elen, & M. J. Bishop (Eds.), *Handbook of research on educational communications and technology* (4th ed.; pp. 239–248). New York: Springer.

USDOE (U.S. Department of Education) (2010). *Transforming American education: Learning powered by technology*. Washington, DC: Office of Education Technology.

Additional Resource

Spector, J. M. (2015). Program evaluation. In J. M. Spector (Ed.), *The SAGE encyclopedia of educational technology* (pp. 593–597). Thousand Oaks, CA: Sage.

twenty-one
Documenting, Reporting and Recommending

When Shakespeare was writing, he wasn't writing for stuff to lie on the page; it was supposed to get up and move around.

(Attributed to Ken Kesey, author of One Flew Over the Cuckoo's Nest)

Educational technology evaluators and evaluation teams have a number of responsibilities, including (a) informing key personnel of how the effort is progressing and the extent to which goals are being attained or are likely to be attained, (b) informing sponsors of how well the effort is progressing and its success or likelihood of success, and (c) informing professional practitioners and scholars of what is working and why as a way to contribute to the knowledge base in a particular area. All of these responsibilities require careful and thorough documentation that will be used in recommendations, reports, presentations and publications.

Some agencies and institutions provide a specific format for evaluation reports. For example, typical things required in an evaluation report to the European Commission of a funded project includes the following:

- a general overview or executive summary with regard to progress;
- a detailed review of interim milestones and deliverables, or final deliverables in the case of a summative evaluation report; this review is required to be specific and link back to the work plan and original proposal; and
- a detailed statement of recommendations for changes to the work plan and/or specific actions to be taken to remedy deficiencies in the case of a formative evaluation, or a detailed statement of the extent to which the project attained intended goals including any additional steps required to correct deficiencies and an overall rating of the effort as deficient, adequate, superior or exceptional.

If no specific format for an evaluation report is required, it is advisable to follow the general format of the *2003 Retrospective Report* and include an executive summary followed by a detailed account of each aspect involved in the evaluation, including what was evaluated, how items to be evaluated were selected, what methods and instruments were used in the evaluation, and how the analysis was conducted.

Components of Evaluation Documentation and Reporting

Typical things to consider when documenting and reporting an evaluation study include:

- the purpose of the report (formative or summative);
- the primary and secondary audiences (those involved in planning and implementation, sponsors, the professional community, etc.);
- an overview or executive summary of the report (since some evaluation reports can be as long as 50 pages or more, a one- to two-page summary will be invaluable to those who have limited time to review all of the details);
- the specific focus and questions addressed in the evaluation study;
- details of the processes developed and used to address those questions;
- details of data sources and instruments used;
- details of analysis methods involved;
- a coherent structure for the report with short syntheses following each critical part of the report;
- a statement of limitations and problems encountered in conducting the study and developing the report; and
- a clear and compelling conclusion of the report including specific recommendations and follow-on actions.

An Example Evaluation Report

Having an exemplar evaluation report to use as a guide for developing an evaluation report is usually a good idea. An excellent one that pertains to an emerging educational technology was completed recently at the National Center for Research on Evaluation, Standards, and Student Testing (CRESST; Chung, Choi, Baker, & Cai, 2014). That report contains an abstract (functions as an overview), an introduction (functions as an executive summary), a methods section, a results section, a summary, references, and appendices containing detailed statistics and a summary of efficacy trial procedures.

Another excellent example of a comprehensive and thorough evaluation report was completed for the U.S. Department of Education's Office of Planning, Evaluation and Policy Development (Bakia, Means, Gallagher, Chen, & Jones, 2009). That 55-page report is organized as follows: executive summary, introduction, technology access, technology-related teacher professional development, integration of technology into instruction, student technology literacy, summary and conclusions, references, and appendices for program administration and data sources and methodology.

Both of these evaluation reports are available on the Internet (see the Links section below). Examining such reports is likely to help an evaluator or evaluation team develop a framework and guidelines pertinent to a particular evaluation of an educational technology effort.

Concluding Thoughts

There has been a great deal of discussion for many years about having educational research influence educational practice in positive and productive ways. An early book aimed at that topic was *Impact of Research on Education: Some Case Studies* (Suppes, 1978). Nine research studies are presented in that volume that had the potential to influence educational practice. However, there is little if any evidence that those exemplary efforts had a sustained impact on a large scale with systemic improvements in educational practice in the USA. Evaluation can and should help bridge the gap between research and practice.

The Theory into Practice Database developed by Greg Kearsley is a good source of information about educational theories and associated research that could and probably should impact learning and instruction in schools and colleges (see www.instructional design.org/about.html). However, that database is primarily used by educational researchers rather than teachers. The Institute of Education Sciences (IES) maintains two sites that potentially could promote dialogue and articulation between researchers and practitioners: (a) the What Works Clearinghouse (see www.ies.ed.gov/ncee/wwc/), and (b) the Educational Resources Information Center (see www.ies.ed.gov/ncee/projects/ eric.asp). Like the Theory into Practice database, both IES sites are used primarily by researchers and have had little impact on the daily practice of teachers.

In short, there is a gap between educational research on learning and instruction and the preparation and practice of teachers. Moreover, there is little support for a link from practice back to research. This situation is aggravated by the explosion of powerful new technologies. Educational technology evaluation is the primary means of bridging that gap. Hopefully, this volume will contribute to improving the links between research and practice in addition to helping guide the work of educational technology evaluators.

Test Your Understanding

Indicate which of the following are examples of responsible evaluation reporting:

a. a verbal debriefing to the leaders of the effort following a key milestone presentation of progress to date;

b. a written report to the sponsors of the project about outcomes attained at the end of the effort;

c. an interview with a news media reporter about the inner workings of the effort;

d. a formal presentation together with project leaders at a national conference; or

e. a private email about strengths and weaknesses of the current effort to a company competing with current project leaders for a follow-on grant.

A Representative Educational Technology Challenge

Suppose you are evaluating an effort involving the introduction of games to support learning mathematics in middle school settings. You might have a look at the CRESST report in Links for such an effort. Feel free to invent another educational technology integration effort or use a different case that might fit your interests. If the evaluation is formative in nature, who would constitute the primary audience for the report? If the evaluation is summative in nature, who would constitute the primary audience for the report? For each kind of evaluation, who might comprise secondary audiences for the report?

Learning Activities

Develop a framework and guidelines for documenting and reporting formative educational technology evaluation efforts. Develop a framework and guidelines for documenting and reporting summative educational technology evaluation efforts.

Links

Evaluation of the enhancing education technology program: Final report (2009)—see www2.ed.gov/rschstat/eval/tech/netts/finalreport.pdf

A randomized evaluation study with innovative impact estimation techniques [CRESST Report 841]—see www.cse.ucla.edu/products/reports/R841.pdf

Greg Kearsley's Research into Practice Database—see www.instructionaldesign.org/about.html

The Educational Resources Information Center—see www.ies.ed.gov/ncee/projects/eric.asp

The What Works Clearinghouse—see www.ies.ed.gov/ncee/projects/eric.asp/

Resources

Basics of good evaluation reporting (University of Wisconsin-Extension, 2002)—see www.uwex.edu/ces/4h/evaluation/documents/Tipsheet14.pdf

Developing an effective evaluation report: Setting the course for effective program evaluation (CDC, 2013)—see www.cdc.gov/eval/materials/developing-an-effective-evaluation-report_tag508.pdf

The Documentation, Monitoring and Evaluation, Reporting, Training, Teamwork, and Supervision (DMERTTS) Framework: Supporting implementation fidelity in community-based settings (Mercy Family Services, 2012)—see www.ausimplementationconference.net.au/presentations/1D-Redshaw.pdf

Growing success: Assessment, evaluation and reporting in Ontario Schools (2010)—see www.edu.gov.on.ca/eng/policyfunding/growSuccess.pdf

How-to Note: Preparing Evaluation Reports (USAID, 2012)—see www.usaid.gov/sites/default/files/documents/1870/How-to-Note_Preparing-Evaluation-Reports.pdf

ICC Evaluation Service: Evaluation Reports—see www.icc-es.org/Evaluation_Reports/

Synergetic Content Creation & Communication: User Evaluation Report (2011)—see www.cordis.europa.eu/docs/projects/cnect/4/231854/080/deliverables/001-sync3d742userevaluationreportv10.pdf

World Education Services Evaluation Reports—see www.wes.org/educators/evalreports.asp

References

Bakia, M., Means, B., Gallagher, L., Chen, E. & Jones, K. (2009). *Evaluation of the enhancing education through technology program: Final report*. Washington, DC: Office of Planning, Evaluation and Policy Development.

Chung, G. K. W. K., Choi, K., Baker, E. L., & Cai, L. (2014). The effects of math video games on learning: A randomized evaluation study with innovative impact estimation techniques [CRESST Report 841]. Los Angeles, CA: CRESST. Retrieved from www.cse.ucla.edu/products/reports/R841.pdf

Suppes, P. (Ed.) (1978). *Impact of research on education: Some case studies*. Washington, DC: National Academy of Education.

part five

ADDITIONAL
RESOURCES

Appendix A:
A Sample
Evaluation
Plan

Sample Evaluation Plan—InvolveMeEarly&Often (IMEO)

The Klingon County Schools Investing in Innovation (i3) InvolveMeEarly&Often (IMEO) five-year project is focusing on integrated data management in support of personalized learning for middle and high school math and reading & language arts students. A critical aspect of this federally funded effort is an ongoing evaluation of the effort. The goal of the effort is to increase graduation rates, decrease drop-out rates, decrease the number and percentage of at-risk/high-need students, and improve test scores of students.

Research suggests that the two critical aspects of achieving these goals are to (1) improve student engagement in learning, and (2) improve teaching focus on instructional support for students. A needs assessment has shown that teachers spend a great deal of time using different administrative and instructional systems, often entering the same information in different systems, which takes time away from teaching activities. In addition, while teachers would like to differentiate instruction for individual and small groups of students with specific needs in accordance with district policy, they are not doing this primarily because they lack the time, expertise and support to do so. As a consequence, this project will create an integrated data management system that directly links the student information system and the learning management system, eliminating the need for multiple data entry of attendance and grades on the part of teachers.

In addition, the new system will support the individual customization of learning based on student past performance and learning preferences through the use of a large repository of learning objects linked to state and national teaching standards and informed with learning analytics that will suggest to teachers which learning objects and learning activities are best suited for individual students, thus relieving teachers of much of the burden of diagnosing learning challenges and suggesting and then developing remediation for individual learners.

The evaluation plan will consist of both formative and summative aspects. The formative evaluation will be based on an ongoing fidelity of implementation study each year that reports on the various activities and professional development planned that year. The summative evaluation will consist of an impact study targeted at the specific goals of the effort—namely, graduate rates, drop-out rates, changes in numbers of high-need students, and student test scores.

The new system will be implemented district-wide at all levels—elementary, middle and high school—and for all subjects. However, the focus is on middle and high schools in the areas of mathematics and English/language arts. A pilot effort in one middle school and one high school for selected math and ELA teachers in year 2 will be the focus of the first fidelity of implementation study and serve as a basis for refining PD and the system. In year 3, half of the remaining middle and high schools will receive and start using the new system, followed by all remaining schools in year 4. This staggered approach allows for refinements in training and in the system and supports a control group study in one year as well as a hierarchical linear method of analysis in years 3, 4 and 5. Duration of exposure to and use of the new system will be a critical factor in analyzing the impact on targeted outcomes. Teacher, student, administrator and parental attitudes and perceptions will be measured throughout the effort.

Program: Klingon County IMEO Logic Model

Situation: FCS has rich data but needs ways to access all data to improve productivity and make instructional decisions at the individual student level

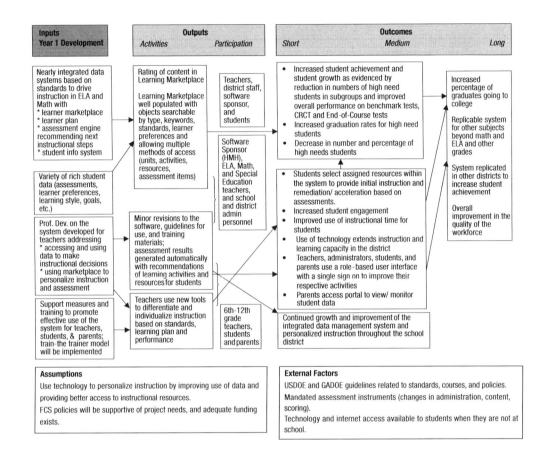

Measuring Fidelity of Implementation: IMEO

Component	Operational definition	Data Collection	Fidelity Scale	Criterion for Adequate/High Fidelity of Implementation
Teacher Professional Development				
1 Cohort 1 (2 pilot schools) Train-the trainer training by HMH Introduction to Pinpoint for Early Implementation (pilot) Schools; the general professional development model used is a train-the-trainer model NOTE: A train-the-trainer has the advantage of developing competence with the new system at FCS	Initial training on Pinpoint delivered by HMH trainers and system experts to district and key school personnel (train the trainer model). The purpose is introduction of Pinpoint, navigation, and basic functions to allow key teachers in pilot schools to begin using the new system	1. Hours of training recorded for each site; 2. Participants recorded (Analyzed as a percentage of the school ELA and math instructional staff) 3. Training materials and training reviewed by key FCS district personnel evaluation team 4. Training materials and training rated by key FCS district personnel 5. Teacher participants rate initial training post training reporting basic knowledge of PinPoint, degree of readiness to independently use Pinpoint, remaining gaps in knowledge 6. Simple knowledge test on use of Pinpoint – 10 items selected by UGA	1. < 3 hours training at the site = 1; 3 – 5 hours training at the site= 2; > 5 or more hours training at the site = 3 2. < 51% participants per school = 1; 51% to 74% participants per school = 2; > 74% participants per school = 3 3. Ratings by evaluation team using a low, medium, high scale 4. Ratings by FCS district personnel using a low, medium, high scale 5. Likert 3-point scale low-medium—high by participating teachers 6. < 5 correct = 1 (low); 5 – 8 correct = 2 (medium); > 8 correct = 3 (high)	3 = high fidelity 2 =medium fidelity 1 = low fidelity NOTES: The scores will be averaged based on equally weighted subscores on a per school bases. Training materials and procedures will be revised and improved based on their use in year two with the pilot schools and district personnel; this is likely to influence this item for cohorts 2 and 3 in subsequent years
Cohort 2 – Initial Training by HMH Delayed implementation so teachers receive no training on Pinpoint initially; start with treatment in year 3				

Cohort 3 – Initial Training by HMH

Delayed implementation so teachers receive no training on Pinpoint initially; start with treatment in year 4; used as a control group in year 3

2 Teacher training in participating schools (in year 2 the two pilot schools; in year 3 half of the remaining schools; in year 4 the remaining half of math and ELA teachers) Training of teachers in the schools that will be implementing the system (math and ELA teachers in middle and high schools; some special education teachers will also be involved) NOTE: in year 2, teacher training will occur in the Fall semester; in subsequent years, some teacher training will occur in the summer before the start of the Fall semester	1. Hours of initial, prescribed training recorded for each site per year Note: This component references the formal training that all teachers initially receive on using the system 2. Participants recorded per year 3. Training materials and training reviewed by evaluation team 4. Training materials and training rated by key FCS district personnel 5. Teacher participants rate initial training post training reporting basic knowledge of PinPoint, degree of readiness to	1. < 3 hours training at the site = 1; 3 – 5 hours training at the site = 2; > 5 or more hours training at the site = 3 2. < 51% participants per school = 1; 51% to 74% participants per school = 2; > 74% participants per school = 3 3. Ratings by evaluation team using a low, medium, high scale 4. Ratings by FCS district personnel using a low, medium, high scale 5. Likert 3-point scale low–medium–high by participating teachers 6. < 5 correct = 1 (low); 5 – 8 correct = 2 (medium); > 8 correct = 3 (high)	3 = high fidelity 2 = medium fidelity 1 = low fidelity NOTES: The scores will be averaged based on equally weighted subscores on a per school bases. Training materials and procedures will be revised and improved based on their use in year two with the pilot schools and district personnel; this is likely to influence this item for cohorts 2 and 3 in subsequent years

continued . . .

Measuring Fidelity of Implementation: IMEO . . . *Continued*

Component	Operational definition	Data Collection	Fidelity Scale	Criterion for Adequate/High Fidelity of Implementation
		independently use Pinpoint, remaining gaps in knowledge 6. Simple knowledge test on use of Pinpoint – 10 items selected by UGA		3 = high fidelity 2 = medium fidelity 1 = low fidelity
3 Individual and small group assistance with the new system by district and school personnel trained in the train-the-trainer activities previously NOTE: in year 2, this only involves the two pilot test schools; remaining schools will be involved in years 3 and 4	Targeted training responsive to specific teacher needs and requirements NOTE: Because a new and complex system is being implemented, it is expected that this kind of training will be ongoing throughout the year and is not an indication of poor initial training in the train-the-trainer approach being adopted; group sessions are considered a positive indicator of teacher collaboration	1. Number of teachers involved per school in additional assistance per year 2. Number of group sessions involved per school 3. Length of training session 4. Evaluation team observe random sessions of assistance 5. Participant feedback on a survey 3 and 6 months after implementation reporting degree of usage and confidence in abilities related to Pinpoint tasks and activities 6. The evaluation team will engage focus groups at each participating school of English and Math teachers; the focus	1. < 51% teachers per school = 1; 51% to 74% teachers = 2; > 74% teachers per school = 3 2. < 3 sessions per school = 1; 3–5 sessions per school = 2; > 5 sessions per school = 3 (Group sessions are considered a positive indicator of teacher collaboration) 3. < 30 minutes per session = 1; 30–50 minutes = 2; > 50 minutes = 3 4. The evaluation team will use a Likert 3-point scale of low-medium-high to rate the assistance sessions in regards to assistance on usage, tasks, and activities 5. Teachers will use a Likert 3-point scale of low-	

		group protocol will solicit feedback on use of system, level of satisfaction, and gaps in knowledge	medium-high with regard to usage, satisfaction, and knowledge gaps 6. Focus Group qualitative data will be quantified using a rubric measuring: (a) extent of usage, (b) satisfaction, and (c) level of knowledge; using a 3-point Likert scale with 1 (low), 2 (medium) and 3 (high) ratings for each area
4 Continued one-on-one technical assistance introducing more complex program components	Ongoing monthly training on an individual basis NOTE: Because a new and complex system is being implemented, it is expected that this kind of training will be ongoing throughout the year and is not an indication of poor initial training in the train-the-trainer approach being adopted	1. Number of teachers involved per school (The number of involved teachers will be recorded each month and a participation percentage calculated by month. The fidelity measure for the year will be based on the grand mean of the monthly averages.) 2. Length of training sessions 3. Ratings of training sessions by evaluation team 4. Ratings by teachers	1. < 51% teachers per school = 1; 51% to 74% teachers = 2; > 74% teachers per school = 3 2. < 30 minutes per session = 1; 30–50 minutes = 2; > 50 minutes = 3 3. The evaluation team will observe random sessions and use a Likert 3-point scale low-medium-high with regard to usage, tasks and activities 4. Teachers will use a Likert 3-point scale low-medium-high with regard to use, satisfaction and 3 = high fidelity 2 = medium fidelity 1 = low fidelity

continued . . .

Measuring Fidelity of Implementation: IMEO ... *Continued*

Component	Operational definition	Data Collection	Fidelity Scale	Criterion for Adequate/High Fidelity of Implementation
		5. Evaluation team will engage focus groups NOTE: Participant feedback on the same surveys and focus groups used for component #3	knowledge gaps. 5. The evaluation team will engage focus groups at each participating school and report on usage, satisfaction and knowledge levels using a 3-point Likert scale with low, medium and high ratings for each area	

Classroom Model

Component	Operational definition	Data Collection	Fidelity Scale	Criterion for Adequate/High Fidelity of Implementation
5 Classroom-implementation of the new system in Math and ELA classrooms	Actual use of the new system by teachers and students on a regular basis with most lessons in the classroom	In classrooms selected randomly by the evaluation team, use of the system by teachers and students observed for major instructional and learning activities 1. Teachers and students use the system on a regular basis as determined by evaluation team observations (2 site visits per school per year; 2 ELA and 2 math observed per visit)	1. Use of system observed in < 75% of the observed classes = 1, 75%–90% of observed classes = 2; > 90% of observed classes = 3 2. < 25% of teachers use the system to create differentiated instruction for groups of students at least once a week = 1; 25–50% of teachers use the system for differentiated instruction at least once a week = 2; > 50% of teachers use	3 = high fidelity 2 = medium fidelity 1 = low fidelity

	2. Use of the system by teachers for differentiated learning 3. Use of the system by teachers for personalized learning NOTE: The existing FCS structured walk-through form approved in the IRB will be used for observations; inconclusive data will be resolved using surveys, focus groups and interview data (IRB procedures approved)	the system for differentiated instruction at least once a week = 3 3. < 25% of teachers use the system to create personalized instruction for groups of students at least once a week = 1; 25%–50% of teachers use the system for personalized instruction at least once a week = 2; > 50% of teachers use the system for personalized instruction at least once a week = 3

Student-Level Model

6 Student engagement with Pinpoint	Use by students of Pinpoint learning activities	1. System logged data on individual student use 2. Reports by student of engagement with Pinpoint on student surveys	1. < 3 hours/week = 1; 3–10 hours/week = 2; > 10 hours/week = 3 2. Data will be derived from student responses on surveys (anticipated > 40% of students will respond to the survey) Survey responses coded to ratings of 1 (low), 2 (medium) and 3 (high) determined by the evaluation team	3 = high fidelity 2 = medium fidelity 1 = low fidelity NOTE: data will be aggregated and averaged as needed to make the above determinations for the fidelity scores for students

continued . . . .

Measuring Fidelity of Implementation: IMEO . . . *Continued*

Component	Operational definition	Data Collection	Fidelity Scale	Criterion for Adequate/High Fidelity of Implementation
School-level Model				
7 School-level support for the new system	Support at each school with a technology integration contact person and one or more teachers trained on the new system	1. Each participating school identifies at least one technical specialist trained on the use of Pinpoint 2. Each participating school identifies at least one Math and one ELA teacher trained on the use of Pinpoint	1. 1 = At least one specialist is present. 0 = No specialist at the school 2. 3 = a math teacher and an ELA teacher have been trained; 2 = either a math teacher or an ELA teacher has been trained; 1 = No teacher has been identified at the school to be trained	1 = high fidelity 0 = low fidelity 3 = high fidelity 2 = medium fidelity 1 = low fidelity
District-level Model				
8 District support for the new system	FCS support for the new system involves developing portals for teachers, students, parents, administrators; and for ensuring that key personnel at FCS are trained to support and maintain the new system	1. FCS portals to support the new system are in place one month prior to school-level implementation 2. FCS personnel trained on the use and maintenance of the new system as observed by the evaluation team and reported by administrator surveys	1. 3 = Portal in place one month prior to implementation 2 = portal in place before the implementation 1 = portal not ready when the implementation should take place 2. Data will be derived from personnel interview responses and feedback on administrator surveys.	3 = high fidelity 2 = medium fidelity 1 = low fidelity 3 = high fidelity 2 = medium fidelity 1 = low fidelity

Qualitative data will be quantified using a 3 point scale of low, medium, and high. Survey responses coded to ratings of 1 (low), 2 (medium) and 3 (high) determined by the evaluation team

Parent-level Model

9 Parental involvement as demonstrated by access to the new system

Parents will have access through a parent portal to the new system (they have had access via a parent portal to the previous Angel system) and the system will log access as before

Data will be collected by FCS on parental access to the system and reported (anonymously) to the evaluation team

< 30% of parents access the system for less than 15 minutes/week = 1 (low); 30 to 60% of parents access the system for more than 15 minutes each/week = 2 (medium); more than 60% of parents access the system for more than 15 minutes/week = 3 (high)

3 = high
2 = medium
1 = low

NOTE: While this is not a fidelity measurement per se, it may help explain the results obtained on other measures data will be aggregated and averaged as needed to make the above determinations for the fidelity score. The scale will be adjusted as required based on FCS historical data (not yet collected) and data on the new system

continued . . . .

Component	Operational definition	Data Collection	Fidelity Scale	Criterion for Adequate/High Fidelity of Implementation
Software-level Model				
10 Software development per requirements of the project	The question addressed here is the extent to which the software partner (HMH) provided the software and associated training per the expectation of the project and key FCS personnel	1. The learning management aspect of Pinpoint was in place one month prior to project use 2. Pinpoint can be used to support differentiated instruction and personalized learning 3. HMH provided timely and appropriate training for key FCS personnel 4. The grade-book and assessments in Pinpoint are automatically linked to the FCS gradebook in use	1. Yes = 1 (adequate) learning management component in place 1 month prior to use; no = 0 (not adequate) component not in place 2. Yes = 1 (adequate) system can be used to support differentiation and personalization; no = 0 (not adequate) differentiation and personalization not possible using the system 3. Yes = 1 (adequate) timely and appropriate training provided; no = 0 (not adequate) the training was not appropriate and/or timely 4. Yes = 1 (adequate) gradebooks linked; no = 0 (not adequate) the Pinpoint gradebook does not link to FCS gradebook in use	1 = adequate 0 = not adequate NOTE: While this is also not a fidelity measure per se, it may help explain the results on other measures. 1 = adequate 0 = not adequate

Impact Study Plan

1 Outcome	2 Name of instrument (and subtest)	3 Test–Retest Reliability	4 Internal Consistency	5 Explanations, notes, comments
Math achievement	Emerald City Middle School Math Assessment (ECMSMA)	0.88	0.90	
Teachers' Math Knowledge	Teacher Math Knowledge Test	0.84	0.89	
Student achievement in LA (CRCT)	Criterion-Referenced Competency Test (CRCT) English Language Arts (state standardized test)	Not reported	Not reported	CRCTs are the state tests for grades 6–8
Student achievement math (state test)	CRCT math (state standardized test)	Not reported	Not reported	CRCTs are the state tests for grades 6–8
Student achievement in LA (EOCT)	End of Course Tests (EOCT) for 9th grade literature and composition and American literature and composition	Not reported	Not reported	EOCTs are the state tests for select courses taken by students in grades 9–12
Student achievement in math (EOCT)	End of Course Tests (EOCT) for Math I and Math II	Not reported	Not reported	EOCTs are the state tests for select courses taken by students in grades 9–12
High school graduation rate	Georgia high school graduation rate	N/A	N/A	

Appendix B: Professional Evaluation Associations

- AEA—The American Evaluation Association; see www.eval.org/
- AECT—The Association for Educational Communications and Technology; see www.aect.org/
- AERA—The American Educational Research Association (several relevant SIGs); see www.aera.net/
- AES—The Australian Evaluation Association; see www.aes.asn.au/
- AfrEA—The African Evaluation Association; see www.afrea.org/
- ASTD/ATD—Association for Talent Development (formerly the American Society for Training Development); see www.astd.org/
- CES—The Canadian Evaluation Society; see www.evaluationcanada.ca/
- CLEAR—Regional Centers for Learning on Evaluation and Results; see www.theclearinitiative.org/index.html
- EARLI—The European Association for Research on Learning and Instruction; see www.earli.org/
- EERA—The European Educational Research Association; see www.eera-ecer.de/
- EERS—Eastern Evaluation Research Society; see www.eers.org/
- EES—The European Evaluation Society; see www.europeanevaluation.org/
- H-PEA—Hawai'i Pacific Evaluation Association; see www.h-pea.org/
- IDEAS—International Development Evaluation Association; see www.unicef.org/evaluation/index_18084.html

- IOCE—International Organization for Cooperation in Evaluation; see www.ioce. net/en/index.php
- IPDET—International Program for Development Evaluation Training (provides links to many evaluation associations); see www.ipdet.org/page.aspx?pageId=links
- ISPI—International Society for Performance Improvement; see www.ispi.org/
- ISTE—International Society for Technology in Education; see www.iste.org/home
- ITEA—International Test and Evaluation Association; see www.itea.org/
- National Technology Leadership Coalition; see www.ntlcoalition.org/
- NEA/AfrEA—Nigerian Evaluation Association; see www.afrea.org/?page=NEA Nigeria
- NWEA—Northwest Evaluation Association; see www.nwea.org/about/
- SEE—Spanish Evaluation Society; see www.sociedadevaluacion.org/
- SEVAL—Swiss Evaluation Association; see www.seval.ch/en/evaluator/index.cfm
- UKES—UK Evaluation Society; see www.evaluation.org.uk/
- WERA—World Educational Research Association; see www.weraonline.org/

Appendix C: Peer-Reviewed Evaluation Journals

- American Journal of Evaluation—see www.aje.sagepub.com/
- Assessment & Evaluation in Higher Education—see www.tandfonline.com/loi/caeh20#.VaqDjC5a1vk
- The Canadian Journal of Program Evaluation—see www.utpjournals.com/The-Canadian-Journal-of-Program-Evaluation
- Educational Researcher—see www.aera.net/pubs/
- Educational Technology Research & Development—see www.springer.com/education+%26+language/learning+%26+instruction/journal/11423
- Educational Technology Review—see www.aace.org/pubs/default.htm
- Educational Technology & Society—see www.ifets.ieee.org/
- Electronic Journal of Information Systems Evaluation—see www.ejise.com/main.html
- Evaluation—see www.evi.sagepub.com/
- Evaluation: The International Journal of Theory, Research and Practice—see www.tavinstitute.org/what-we-offer/journals/evaluation-the-international-journal-of-theory-research-and-practice/
- Evaluation and Program Planning—see www.sciencedirect.com/science/journal/01497189
- The Journal of Applied Instructional Design—see www.jaidpub.org/

- Journal of MultiDisciplinary Evaluation—see www.journals.sfu.ca/jmde/index.php/jmde_1
- Journal of Research on Technology in Education—see www.iste.org/Content/NavigationMenu/Publications/JRTE/Issues/Volume42/Number3Spring2010/JRTE_Volume_42_Number_3_Spring_2010.htm
- Journal of Testing and Evaluation—see www.astm.org/DIGITAL_LIBRARY/JOURNALS/TESTEVAL/
- Instructional Science—see www.springer.com/education+%26+language/learning+%26+instruction/journal/11251
- International Journal of Designs for Learning—see www.scholarworks.iu.edu/journals/index.php/ijdl/index
- International Journal of Evaluation and Research in Education—see www.iaesjournal.com/online/index.php/IJERE
- New Directions for Evaluation—see www.onlinelibrary.wiley.com/journal/10.1002/(ISSN)1534-875X/issues
- Performance Improvement Quarterly—see www.ispi.org/
- Practical Assessment, Research & Evaluation—see www.pareonline.net/
- Research Evaluation—see www.rev.oxfordjournals.org/
- Review of Research in Education—www.aera.net/pubs/
- TechTrends—see www.link.springer.com/journal/11528

Glossary
of Terms

(starred items are from the *Foundations* volume)

*Competency: a related set of knowledge, skills and attitudes that are associated with successful performance of a task or job function.

*Education: processes involved in improving knowledge, performance and understanding through systematic and sustained efforts.

Educational intervention: a planned effort to introduce a change that is likely to result in desired outcomes.

Educational policy: a set of mandated activities, procedures, regulations or standards that govern the conduct of various educational tasks.

Educational practice: a set of activities or procedures that are normally carried out in association with an educational task.

Educational product: a designed artifact that is intended to improve learning, performance and/or instruction.

Educational program: a planned effort with high-level educational goals that has (or had) a definite beginning and is expected to continue, possibly with changes and refinements, for an indefinite period of time.

Educational project: a planned effort to bring about desired educational outcomes that has a budget, resources, a definite beginning, a duration, and reasonably well-defined goals and objectives.

Evaluation: a process aimed at improving or determining the value and quality of a goal-driven effort; evaluations may be *formative* and aimed at improving the effort or *summative* and aimed at providing an overall judgment about the value of the effort.

Fidelity of implementation: a study of how well an effort is being designed and developed; a kind of formative evaluation that focuses on the inputs and outputs columns in the logic model that is often a mixed methods study.

*Formative assessment: a process typically involving timely and informative feedback to a learner so as to improve the learner's performance and understanding.

Formative evaluation: an evaluation of an effort that is aimed primarily at improving the effort as it evolves so as to ensure the greatest possible degree of success; a fidelity of implementation study is a common form of formative evaluation.

Impact study: a kind of summative evaluation that focuses on the outcomes of an effort; a primarily quantitative study that should link back to the initial concerns and goals of the effort.

Inputs: the part of a logic model that includes activities in support of the design, development and deployment of an educational technology effort; inputs typically include such things as resources required and obtained, training materials developed, training provided, results of quality reviews and small-scale field tests, and so on.

*Instruction: that which facilitates and supports learning.

*Intentional learning: goal-directed learning; learning that is planned and purposeful.

*Learning: a process that results in stable and persisting changes in a person's abilities, attitudes, beliefs, knowledge, mental models, and/or skills.

*Learning types: the different kinds of things that can be learned, such as attitudes, concepts, motor skills, principles, rules, skills, etc.

Logic model: a visual representation of the theory of change for a particular effort that depicts (a) key aspects of the current situation, (b) activities associated with the effort (inputs), (c) the anticipated results of those activities (outputs), and (d) short-, medium-, and long-term outcomes of the effort.

Mediator variable: a variable that explains the relationship between an independent and a dependent variable or whether or not a relationship exists.

*Mental models: internal representations of experience that are created just when needed to explain unusual phenomena or solve challenging problems.

Moderator variable: a variable that affects the director or strength of the relationship between an independent and a dependent variable.

Needs assessment: a specific and systematic set of procedures used to identify problems and underlying causes, and set priorities for decisions about planned actions or improvements and associated resource allocations.

Outputs: that column in a logic model that focuses on the results of the activities and processes depicted in the inputs column; these results comprise a major portion of a fidelity of implementation study or other form of formative evaluation.

*Performance: an observable behavior or action that serves as an indicator of competence or mastery of a learning task.

Policy: a formal statement of an institution that is intended to mandate specific activities and practices with regard to various situations for a variety of purposes; policies are often developed in support of a mission or vision statement.

Practice: an established pattern of behavior in various situations and circumstances that may be incorporated in the form of policy guidelines, procedures or standards.

Product: a designed object or artifact that has an intended use and purpose.

Program: an ongoing collection of related activities and resources with a particular goal and set of resources and constraints.

Project: an effort with goals and objectives that has a definitive beginning and end.

Reliability: the degree to which consistent and stable results are found (alternatively, the degree to which the thing being done is being done or was done well).

*Summative assessment: a process involving a formal report of an individual's level of performance and understanding in terms of a set of established standards.

Summative evaluation: an evaluation study that reports the extent to which an effort has achieved its intended efforts; an impact study is a common form of summative evaluation; a summative evaluation focuses on the outcomes columns in the logic model in light of the initial problem or situation.

System dynamics: the study of complex systems that have many interrelated and interacting components with some non-linear relationships and which often have delayed effects when a change is implemented; educational systems are complex, dynamic systems.

*__Technology__: the practical and purposeful application of knowledge.

__Theory of change__: an explanation of how and why a particular effort can be expected to resolve a problematic situation or transform the current state of affairs into a desired state of affairs; a theory of change can be visually represented in a logic model.

__Validity__: the degree to which what is measured or reported is representative of what was intended to be measured or reported (alternatively, the degree to which the right thing is being done or was done).

Consolidated
References

Anderson, S. W. & Young, S. M. (1999). The impact of contextual and process factors on the evaluation of activity-based costing systems. *Accounting, Organizations and Society, 24*, pp. 525–559.

Arthur, J., Waring, M., Coe, R., & Hedges, L. V. (2012). *Research methods & methodologies in education.* Thousand Oaks, CA: Sage Publications.

Bakia, M., Means, B., Gallagher, L., Chen, E., & Jones, K. (2009). *Evaluation of the enhancing education through technology program: Final report.* Washington, DC: Office of Planning, Evaluation and Policy Development.

Baron, R. M., & Kenny, D. A. (1986). The moderator–mediator variable distinction in social psychological research: Conceptual, strategic, and statistical considerations. *Journal of Personality and Social Psychology, 51*, 1173–1182.

Bates, R. (2004). A critical analysis of evaluation practice: The Kirkpatrick model and the principle of beneficence. *Evaluation and Program Planning, 27*(3), 341–347.

Benjamin, S. (1989). A closer look at needs analysis and needs assessment: Whatever happened to the systems approach? *Nonprofit Management Leadership, 28*, 12–16.

Black, P., & Wiliam, D. (1998). Assessment and classroom learning. *Assessment in Education: Principles, Policy & Practice, 5*(1), 7–71.

Blumenfeld, P. C., Soloway, E., Marx, R. W., Krajcik, J. S., Guzdial, M., & Palincsar, A. (1991). Motivating project-based learning: Sustaining the doing, supporting the learning. *Educational Psychologist, 26*(3&4), 369–398. Retrieved from www.academia.edu/2487241/Motivating_project-based_learning_Sustaining_the_doing_supporting_the_learning

Burns, R. (1795). To a mouse, on turning up in her nest with the plough. Retrieved from www.poetry foundation.org/poem/173072

Carroll, C., Patterson, M., Wood, S., Booth, A., Rick, J., & Balain, S. (2007). A conceptual framework for implementation fidelity. *Implementation Science, 2*(1), 40–49. Retrived from www.implementation science.com/content/pdf/1748-5908-2-40.pdf

Chen, H.-T. (2005). Theory-driven evaluation. In S. Mathison (Ed.), *Encyclopedia of evaluation* (pp. 415–419). Thousand Oaks, CA: Sage. Retrieved from www.srmo.sagepub.com/view/encyclopedia-of-evaluation/n542.xml

Chung, G. K. W. K., Choi, K., Baker, E. L., & Cai, L. (2014). The effects of math video games on learning: A randomized evaluation study with innovative impact estimation techniques [CRESST Report 841]. Los Angeles, CA: CRESST. Retrieved from www.cse.ucla.edu/products/reports/R841.pdf

Collins, A., Brown, J. S., & Newman, S. E. (1987). *Cognitive apprenticeship: Teaching the craft of reading, writing, and mathematics* [BBN Technical Report #403]. Champaign, IL: University of Illinois at Urbana-Champaign. Retrieved from www.ideals.illinois.edu/bitstream/handle/2142/17958/ctrstread techrepv01987i00403_opt.pdf?sequence=1

Collins, J. (2005). *Good to great and the social sectors: A monography to accompany Good to Great.* New York: Harper.

Cook, T. D., & Campbell, D. T. (1979). *Quasi-experimentation: Design and analysis issues for field settings.* Boston, MA: Houghton Mifflin.

Crawford, L., Carpenter II, D. M., Wilson, M. T., Schmeister, M., & McDonald, M. (2012). Testing the relation between fidelity of implementation and student outcomes in math. *Assessment for Effective Intervention, 37*(4), 224–2325.

Crewsell, J. W., & Clark, V. L. P. (2011). *Designing and conducting mixed methods research* (2nd ed.). Thousand Oaks, CA: Sage Publications.

CTGV (Cognition and Technology Group at Vanderbilt) (1990). Anchored instruction and its relationship to situated cognition. *Educational Researcher, 19*(6), 2–10. Retrieved from www.calteach.ucsc.edu/aboutus/documents/AnchoredInstruction.pdf

Culp, K. M., Honey, M., & Mandinach, E. (2003). *A retrospective on twenty years of educational technology policy.* Washington, DC: Office of Educational Technology. Retrieved from www2.ed.gov/rschstat/eval/tech/20years.pdf

Dane, A. V., & Schneider, B. H. (1988). Program integrity and early secondary prevention: Are implementation efforts out of control? *Clinical Psychology Review, 18*(1), 23–45.

Davern, M. D. (2008). Representative sample. In P. J. Lavrakas (Ed.), *Encyclopedia of survey research methods* (pp. 721–723). Thousand Oaks, CA: Sage Publications.

Davis, R., Misra, S., & van Auken, S. (2002). A gap analysis approach to marketing curriculum assessment: A study of skills and knowledge. *Journal of Marketing Education, 24*(3), 218–224. Retrieved from www.jmd.sagepub.com/content/24/3/218.short

Dewey, J. (1938). *Experience & education.* New York: Touchstone/Kappa Delta Pi. Retrieved from www.ruby.fgcu.edu/courses/ndemers/colloquium/experienceeducationdewey.pdf

Dörner, D. (1996). *The logic of failure: Why things go wrong and what we can do to make them right,* trans. R. & R. Kimber. New York: Henry Holt & Co.

Durand, R., Decker, P. J., & Kirkman, D. M. (2014). Evaluation methodologies for estimating the likelihood of program implementation failure. *American Journal of Evaluation, 35*(3), 404–418.

Dusenbury, L., Brannigan, R., Falco, M., & Hansen, W. B. (2003). A review of research on fidelity of implementation: Implications for drug abuse prevention in school settings. *Health Education Research, 18*(2), 237–256.

Ellsworth, J. B. (2015). Change agency. In J. M. Spector (Ed.), *The SAGE encyclopedia of educational technology* (pp. 97–100). Thousand Oaks, CA: Sage Publications.

Fitzpatrick, J. L., Sanders, J. R., & Worthen, B. R. (2011). *Program evaluation: alternative approaches and practical guidelines* (4th ed.). Upper Saddle River, NJ: Pearson Education.

Gagné, R. M. (1968). Learning hierarchies. *Educational Psychologist, 6*(1), 1–9.

Gagné, R. M. (1985). *The conditions of learning and theory of instruction* (4th ed.). New York: Holt, Rinehart & Winston.

Gagné, R. M., & Merrill, M. D. (1990). Integrative goals for instructional design. *Educational Technology Research and Development, 38*(1), 23–30.

Gibbons, A. S. (2014). *An architectural approach to instructional design*. New York: Routledge.

Greene, J. C., Caracelli, V. J., & Graham, W. F. (1989). Toward a conceptual framework for mixed-methods evaluation designs. *Educational Evaluation and Policy Analysis, 11*(3), 255–274.

Griffith, T. L. (2012). *The plugged-in manager: Get in tune with your people, technology, and organization to thrive*. San Francisco, CA: Jossey-Bass.

Halff, H. M. (1993). Prospects for automating instructional design. In J. M. Spector, M. C. Polson, & D. J. Muraida (Eds.), *Automating instructional design: Concepts and issues* (pp. 67–131). Englewood Cliffs, NJ: Educational Technology Publications.

Hamilton, J., & Feldman, J. (2014). Planning a program evaluation: Matching methodology to program status. In J. M. Spector, M. D. Merrill, J. Elen, & M. J. Bishop (Eds.), *Handbook of research on educational communications and technology* (4th ed., pp. 249–256). New York: Springer.

Harris, P., & Walling, D. R. (2014). Policies governing educational technology practice and research. In J. M. Spector, M. D. Merrill, J. Elen, & M. J. Bishop (Eds.), *Handbook of research on educational communications and technology* (4th ed.; pp. 627–640). New York, NY: Springer.

Harvey, A., & Kamvounias, P. (2007). Bridging the implementation gap: A teacher-as-learner approach to teaching and learning policy. *Higher Education Research & Development, 27*(1), 31–41.

Herring. M. C., & Smaldino, S. E. (2015). TPACK (Technological Pedagogical Content Knowledge): Implications for 21st century education. In J. M. Spector (Ed.), *The SAGE encyclopedia of educational technology* (pp. 785–787). Thousand Oaks, CA: Sage.

Huber, V. L., & Gay, G. (1984). Use of educational technology for formative evaluation. *New Directions for Adult and Continuing Education, 24*(1), 55–64.

Johnson, R. B., & Onwuegbuzie, A. J. (2004). Mixed methods research: A research paradigm whose time has come. *Educational Researcher, 33*(7), 14–26.

Kirkpatrick, D. L. (1959). Techniques for evaluating training programs. *Journal of the American Society of Training Directors, 13*(3), 21–26.

Kirschner, P. A., Sweller, J., & Clark, R. E. (2006). Why minimal guidance during instruction does not work: An analysis of the failure of constructivist, discovery, problem-based, experiential, and inquiry-based teaching. *Educational Psychologist, 4*(2) 75–86. Retrieved from www.projects.ict.usc.edu/itw/vtt/Constructivism_Kirschner_Sweller_Clark_EP_06.pdf

Kozma, R. B., & Vota, W. S. (2014). ICT in developing countries: Policies, implementation and impact. In J. M. Spector, M. D. Merrill, J. Elen, & M. J. Bishop (Eds.), *Handbook of research on educational communications and technology* (4th ed.; pp. 885–894). New York: Springer.

Lave, J., & Wenger, E. (1990). *Situated learning: Legitimate peripheral participation*. Cambridge, UK: Cambridge University Press.

Lincoln, Y. S., & Guba, E. G. (2000). Paradigmatic controversies, contradictions and emerging confluences. In N. K. Denzin & Y. S. Lincoln (Eds.), *Handbook of qualitative research* (2nd ed.; pp. 163–188). Thousand Oaks, CA: Sage.

Luschei, T. F. (2014). Assessing the costs and benefits of educational technology. In J. M. Spector, M. D. Merrill, J. Elen, & M. J. Bishop (Eds.), *Handbook of research on educational communications and technology* (4th ed.; pp. 239–248). New York: Springer.

Lynn, G. (2014). Revising an engineering design rubric: A case study illustrating principles and practices to ensure technical quality of rubrics. *Practical Assessment, Research & Evaluation, 19*(8). Retrieved from www.pareonline.net/getvn.asp?v=19&n=8

McCawley, P. F. (2009). Methods for conducting an educational needs assessment: Guidelines for cooperative extensive system professionals. Moscow, ID: University of Idaho. Retrieved from www.cals.uidaho.edu/edcomm/pdf/BUL/BUL0870.pdf

McKillip, J. (1998). Need analysis: Process and techniques. In L. Bickman & D. J. Rog (Eds.), *Handbook of applied social research methods* (pp. 261–284). Thousand Oaks, CA: Sage.

McLaughlin, J. A., & Jordan, G.B. (2010), Using logic models. In J. S. Wholey, H. P. Hatry & K. E. Newcomer (Eds.), *Handbook of practical program evaluation*, (3rd ed.; pp 62–87). Hoboken, NJ: John Wiley & Sons.

Mertens, D. M., & Wilson, A. T. (2012). *Program evaluation theory and practice: A comprehensive guide*. New York: Guilford Press.

Milrad, M., Spector, J. M., & Davidsen, P. I. (2003). Model facilitated learning. In S. Naidu (Ed.), *Learning and teaching with technology: Principles and practices* (pp. 13–27). London: Kogan Page.

Mishra, P., & Koehler, M. J. (2006). Technological pedagogical content knowledge: A framework for teacher knowledge. *Teacher College Record, 108*(6), 1017–1054.

Moeller, B., & Reitzes, T. (2011). *Integrating technology with student-centered learning*. Report to the Nellie Mae Education Foundation. Quincy, MA: Nellie Mae Foundation. Retrieved from www.nme foundation.org/getmedia/befa9751-d8ad-47e9-949d-bd649f7c0044/integrating

Norman, D. A. (1988). *The design of everyday things*. New York: Basic Books.

OME (2001). Comprehensive needs assessment. Retrieved from www2.ed.gov/admins/lead/account/compneedsassessment.pdf

Oppenheim, A. N. (1992). *Questionnaire design and attitude measurement*. London: Pinter Publishers.

Owston, R. (2007). Contextual factors that sustain innovative pedagogical practice using technology: An international study. *Journal of Educational Change, 8*(1), 61–77.

Owston, R. (2008). Models and methods for evaluation. In J. M. Spector, M. D. Merrill, J. J. G. van Merriënboer, & M. P. Driscoll (Eds.), *Handbook of research on educational communications and technology* (3rd ed.; pp. 605–617). New York: Routledge.

Petrosino, A. (2000). Answering the why question in evaluation: The causal-model approach. *Canadian Journal of Program Evaluation, 15*(1), 1–24.

Pintrich, P. R., Marx, R. W., & Boyle, R. A. (1993). Beyond cold conceptual change: The role of motivational beliefs and classroom contextual factors in the process of conceptual change. *Review of Educational Research, 63*(2), 167–199.

Portenoy, R. K., Thaler, H. T., Kornblith, A. B., Lepore, J. M., Friedlander-Klar, H., Kiyasu, E., Sobel, K., Coyle, N., Kemeny, N., Norton, L. & Scher, H. (1994).The memorial symptom assessment scale: An instrument for the evaluation of symptom prevalence, characteristics and distress. *European Journal of Cancer, 30A*(9), 1326–1336.

Project Management Institute (2013). *A guide to the project management body of knowledge* (5th ed.). Newtown Square, PA: Project Management Institute.

Reigeluth, C. M., & Stein, F. S. (1983). The elaboration theory of instruction. In C. M. Reigeluth (Ed.), *Instructional-design theories and models: An overview of their current status* (pp. 338–381). Hillsdale, NJ: Erlbaum.

Reviere, R., Berkowitz, Carter, C. C., & Ferguson, C. G. (Eds.) (2008). *Needs assessment: A creative and practice guide for social scientists*. New York: Routledge.

Riasat, A., Rizvi S. S., Zehara, F., & Arain, F. (2008). The role of system dynamics in learning environments. In M. Iskander (Ed.), *Innovative techniques in instruction technology technology, e-learning, and education* (pp. 538–541). New York, NY: Springer.

Richey, R. C., Klein, J. D., & Tracey, M. W. (2011). *The instructional design knowledge base: Theory, research and practice*. New York: Routledge.

Rogers, E. M. (2003). *Diffusion of innovations* (5th ed.). New York: Simon & Schuster.

Rogers, P. J. (2007). Theory-based evaluation: Reflections ten years on. In Mathison, S. (Ed.), *Enduring issues in evaluation: The 20th anniversary of the collaboration between NDE and AEA*. New directions for evaluation. Vol. 114 (pp. 63–67). San Francisco, CA: Jossey-Bass Publishers and the American Evaluation Association.

Rogers, P. J., Petrosino, A., Huebner, T. A., & Hacsi, T. A. (2000). Program theory evaluation: Practice, promise, and problems. *New directions for evaluation, 2000*(87), 5–13.

Rooney, J. J., & Heuvel, L. N. V. (2004). Root cause analysis for beginners. *Quality Progress*, July, 45–53. Retrieved from https://servicelink.pinnacol.com/pinnacol_docs/lp/cdrom_web/safety/management/accident_investigation/Root_Cause.pdf

Ross, S. M., & Morrison, G. R. (1995). Evaluation as a tool for research and development: Issues and trends in its applications in educational Technology. In R. D. Tennyson & A. E. Barron (Eds.), *Automating instructional design: Computer-based development and delivery tools* (pp. 491–522). New York: Springer.

Rossett, A. (2009). *First things fast: A handbook for performance analysis* (2nd ed.). San Francisco, CA: John Wiley & Sons.

Ruiz-Primo, M. A. (2005, April). A multi-method and multi-source approach for studying fidelity of implementation. Paper presented at the AERA Annual Meeting, Montreal, Canada, April 14, 2005.

Scandura, J. M. (1970). The role of rules in behavior: Toward an operational definition of what (rule) is learned. *Psychological Review, 77,* 516–533.

Schifferdecker, K. E., & Reed, V. A. (2009). Using mixed methods research in medical education: Basic guidelines for researchers. *Medical Education, 43*(7), 637–644.

Schröter, D. C., Magura, S., & Coryn, C. (2015). Deconstructing evidence-based practice: Progress and ambiguities. *Evaluation and Program Planning, 48*(1), 90–91.

Smith, C. D. (2008). Design focused evaluation. *Assessment & Evaluation in Higher Education, 33*(6), 631–645.

Spector, J. M. (2012). *Foundations of educational technology: Integrative approaches and interdisciplinary perspectives.* New York: Routledge.

Spector, J. M. (2014). Program and project evaluation. In J. M. Spector, M. D. Merrill, J. Elen, & M. J. Bishop (Eds.). *Handbook of research on educational communications and technology* (4th ed.; pp. 195–201). New York: Springer.

Spector, J. M. (2015). *Foundations of educational technology: Integrative approaches and interdisciplinary perspectives* (2nd ed.). New York: Routledge.

Spector, J. M. (2015). Program evaluation. In J. M. Spector (Ed.), *The SAGE encyclopedia of educational technology* (pp. 593–597). Thousand Oaks, CA: Sage.

Spector, J. M. (2015). System dynamics. In J. M. Spector (Ed.), *The SAGE encyclopedia of educational technology* (pp. 693–697). Thousand Oaks, CA: Sage Publications.

Spector, J. M. (2015). The changing nature of educational technology programs. *Educational Technology, 55*(2), 19–25.

Spector, J. M., Polson, M. C., & Muraida, D. J. (Eds.) (1993). *Automating instructional design: Concepts and issues.* Englewood Cliffs, NJ: Educational Technology.

Spector, J. M., Johnson, T. E., & Young, P. A. (2014). An editorial on research and development in and with educational technology. *Educational Technology Research & Development, 62*(2), 1–12.

Sterman, J. D. (1994). Learning in and about complex systems. *System Dynamics Review, 10*(2–3), 291–330.

Sullivan, L. H. (1924). *Autobiography of an idea.* New York: Press of the American Institute of Architectures.

Suppes, P. (Ed.) (1978). *Impact of research on education: Some case studies.* Washington, DC: National Academy of Education.

Sweller, J., van Merriënboer, J. J. G., & Paas, F. G. W. C. (1998), Cognitive architecture and instructional design. *Educational Psychology Review, 10*(3), 251–296.

Tennyson, R. D. (1995). Instructional systems development: The fourth generation. In Tennyson, R. D. & Barron, A. (Eds.), *Automating instructional design: Computer-based development and delivery tools* (pp. 33–78). New York: Springer.

United Nations Development Fund for Women (UNIFEM). (2009, July). *EU gender politics in an international context—Gender perspectives and gender indicators* [Report from the international WOMNET conference]. Berlin: United Nations Development Fund.

USDOE (U.S. Department of Education) (2010). *Transforming American education: Learning powered by technology.* Washington, DC: Office of Education Technology.

van Merriënboer, J. J. G. (1997). *Training complex cognitive skills: A four-component instructional design model for technical training.* Englewood Cliffs, NJ: Educational Technology Publications.

Watkins, R., & Kaufman, R. (1996). An update of relating needs assessment and needs analysis. *Performance Improvement Journal, 35*(10), 10–13.

Weiss, C. H. (1972). *Evaluation research. Methods for assessing program effectiveness.* Englewood Cliffs, NJ: Prentice-Hall.

Weiss, C. H. (1997). Theory-based evaluation: Past, present, and future. *New Directions for Evaluation, 76,* 41–55.

Weston, T. (2004). Formative evaluation for implementation: Evaluating educational technology applications and lessons. *American Journal of Evaluation, 25*(1), 51–64.

White, R. T., & Arzi, H. J. (2005). Longitudinal studies: Design, validity, practicality, and value. *Research in Science Education, 35*(1), 137–149.

Wiersma, W. (1995). *Research methods in education* (6th ed.). Boston, MA: Allyn & Bacon.

Witkin, B. R., & Altschuld, J. W. (1995). *Planning and conducting needs assessments: A practical guide.* Thousand Oaks, CA: Sage.

W. K. Kellogg Foundation (2004). Using logic models to bring together planning, evaluation, and action: Logic model development guide. Battle Creek, MI: W. K. Kellogg Foundation. Retrieved from www.smartgivers.org/uploads/logicmodelguidepdf.pdf

Zikmund, W. (1997). *Business research methods* (5th ed.). Orlando, FL: Harcourt College.

Additional References

Altschuld, J. W., & Kumar, D. D. (2010). *The needs assessment KIT—Book 1, needs assessment: An overview.* Thousand Oaks, CA: SAGE Publications.

Anderson, L. W., & Postlethwaite, T. N. (2007). *Program evaluation: Large-scale and small-scale studies.* Brussels, Belgium: The International Academy of Education and the International Institute for Education. Retrieved from www.unesdoc.unesco.org/images/0018/001817/181752e.pdf

Kaufman, R. (1988). Preparing useful performance indicators. *Training and Development Journal, 42*(9), 80–83.

Kaufman, R., & English, F. W. (1979). *Needs assessment: Concept and application.* Englewood Cliffs, NJ: Educational Technology Publications.

Kaufman, R., Rojas, A., & Mayer, H. (1993). *Needs assessment: A user's guide.* Englewood Cliffs, NJ: Educational Technology Publishers.

Kaufman, R., Keller, J., & Watkins, R. (1996). What works and what doesn't: Evaluation beyond Kirkpatrick. *Performance+ Instruction, 35*(2), 8–12.

Taplin, D, H., Clark, H., Collins, E., & Colby, D. C. (2013). *Theory of change: Technical papers.* New York: ActKnowledge.

Watkins, R. & Kaufman, R. (2002). Assessing and Evaluating: Differentiating perspectives. *Performance Improvement Journal, 41*(2), 22–28.

Watkins, R., West Meiers, M. & Visser, Y. (2012). *A guide to assessing needs: Tools for collecting information, making decisions, and achieving development results.* Washington, DC: World Bank.

Index